An/Other Praxis

An/Other
PRAXIS

A Critical Option for Ecclesial Freedom

HERRY M. MUKDANI

WIPF & STOCK · Eugene, Oregon

AN/OTHER PRAXIS
A Critical Option for Ecclesial Freedom

Copyright © 2013 Herry M. Mukdani. All rights reserved. Except for brief quotations in critical publications or reviews, no part of this book may be reproduced in any manner without prior written permission from the publisher. Write: Permissions, Wipf and Stock Publishers, 199 W. 8th Ave., Suite 3, Eugene, OR 97401.

Scriptures taken from the Holy Bible, New International Version®, NIV®. Copyright © 1973, 1978, 1984, 2011 by Biblica, Inc.™ Used by permission of Zondervan. All rights reserved worldwide.www.zondervan.com The "NIV" and "New International Version" are trademarks registered in the United States Patent and Trademark Office by Biblica, Inc.™

Wipf and Stock
An Imprint of Wipf and Stock Publishers
199 W. 8th Ave., Suite 3
Eugene, OR 97401

www.wipfandstock.com

ISBN 13: 978-1-62564-255-4

Manufactured in the U.S.A.

In memory of my parents

Ibrahim Mukdani
(1933–1977)
Martha *Wis* Nusah
(1936–1972)

Who, by example,
showed me how fragile their identities were
as they moved into borderlands
crisscrossed with a variety of
languages, experiences, and voices
in order to open diverse cultural spaces to others,
and led me on the quest to know more *Otherness*.

Contents

Note to the Reader   ix

Acknowledgments   xi

Introduction: Political Eschatology from the Underside by Theodore W. Jennings Jr.   xiii

1   Situating Ecclesial Praxis Today   1
2   Re-imagining Ecclesia of Freedom   17
3   Naming the Subaltern   33
4   Crossing Borders Intellectually   47
5   The *Dhalang* Roles for Transformative Ritual Leadership   79

Bibliography   101

Note to the Reader

This book is one of constructive suggestions for ecclesial praxis today. It does not simply address the fact that colonialism was cultural and epistemic, or challenge the existing colonial legacy. Rather, it requires us to move away from monolingual and monological understandings of liberation and move toward an inclusive divers(al)ity that incorporates the contributions of all marginalized groups. This critical engagement, which mixes with multiple struggles, is intended to create a little more space to imagine that both an alternative world and a different system of knowing are possible.

      Christians must acknowledge that what our theological projects and Christian ministries of the past centuries left behind are the crises of humanity. Human beings have increasingly suffered in this world, from wars, persecution, globalized poverty, and more. In looking back at what Christianity has done, I have discovered that neither theologians nor Christian churches claimed their success in the face of this crisis of humanity. God calls us to continue the struggle of searching for those who suffer, of doing theology from the undersides of history, and of bringing humanity back together to live in harmony.

Acknowledgments

I WOULD LIKE TO express my gratitude to friends, colleagues, and faculty members of religious "Leaders for the Next" at Chicago Theological Seminary and Chicago Metropolitan Association, United Church of Christ, with whom I have been able to write constructive discussions on theology, ethics, and human sciences. I especially thank Rev. Kim Chul-Gu, a faculty member at GIDI Theological Seminary in Papua, Indonesia.

On a personal note, I could not have completed this project without the ongoing support of a number of close friends and family, and to them I am grateful. I would like to thank to my older brother, Tommy Mukdani, for his support. Also I need to mention Dick and Gay Harter, Walt and Bev Watts, Dennis, Twila, and Marjorie Carlson for being such good friends and family.

I give thanks to the special people in my life—my wife, Engeline, and my son, Liberio, to whom I am ever thankful and to whom I dedicate this book.

Introduction

Political Eschatology from the Underside

IN THIS VERY FINE and provocative study, Herry Mukdani points the way forward into an ecclesial praxis that takes seriously the situatedness of the community within a wider society and that accentuates the border-crossing and subaltern perspective of those who are marginalized under the ruling order. In the course of his argument, Mukdani rightly refers to the eschatological, and indeed, political-eschatological character of the Christian message.

In this essay—in place of a foreword—I want to give some background to this question of hope, a hope that is not based on an overarching view of the "progress" of "civilization" that, as Mukdani has noted, has long served as the basis for imperialisms, colonialisms, and neocolonialisms. Instead it is a hope rooted in the yearnings of the lowly, the disinherited, and the marginalized. It is in the context of a hope such as this that communities of subaltern Christians may engage in an ecclesial praxis that does not separate them from their social world, but instead enables them to

Introduction

work in open collaboration towards a common life of justice, generosity, and joy.

In order to do this, I want to indicate something of how approaches to the apocalyptic have been characterized through several turns in twentieth-century theology.

In 1892, the son-in-law of the great liberal theologian Albrecht Ritschl published his monograph on the preaching of Jesus on the reign of God. The idea of the kingdom of God had been a mainstay of liberal theology in the nineteenth century. In one way or another, with greater or lesser degrees of sophistication, the theme or motif of the kingdom of God in the teaching and preaching of Jesus had enabled liberal theology to seek a certain synthesis between the project of Western progress and the essence of Christianity.

Johannes Weiss was a product of this theological current. But he was also a product of another facet of liberal theology: the historical critical approach to the study of biblical texts. It was in this vocation that Weiss shattered the theological foundation of liberal theology, for he demonstrated that Jesus' preaching on the kingdom of God had nothing to do with the progressive reform of civilization, nor with the awakening of a consciousness of the love of God and neighbor as the interior realization of the kingdom of God. Rather, that preaching had in view the impending catastrophe of world civilization, the collapse of all structures of the world under the impact of the immediate coming of God's reign as a universal kingdom of divine justice. His preaching was therefore like that of one who sees a coming catastrophe and cries "Look out!" Of course, this was good news, since Jesus saw a new world taking the place of the old, one in which the excluded, the impoverished, and the marginalized would find community.

Introduction

Weiss' view was taken up by Albert Schweitzer, who recognized that this apocalyptic consciousness stood in fatal contrast to our own world.[1] The end of the ages had not come, and this provoked a crisis in appropriating Jesus for the tasks of living in the modern age.

It was hard to know what to do with Jesus as a preacher of the imminent end of history until the coming of the First World War, when the entire project of Western European civilization ran into the abyss. The liberal progressive synthesis of Christianity with Western culture went over the cliff as leading Christian intellectuals such as Harnack endorsed the war policies of Germany (and of course something similar happened in other nations entangled in this web). The young Karl Barth, together with other theologians of his generation, including Gogarten, Bultmann, and Tillich, suddenly found in the apocalyptic of Jesus and Paul a word of illumination, like lightening flashing in the dark, stormy night of Europe's fatal agony. In reading the early texts of these emerging dialectical theologians in the aftermath of the war, one sees the affirmation of the gospel as entailing the catastrophe of what had called itself Western civilization.

Christ is the crisis of civilization, of culture, of religion, even of what is called Christianity. But what does this mean, and how is it to be thought of? In answer came Kierkegaard's infinite qualitative distinction between time and eternity as the intersection and irresolvable coincidence of opposites—the eternal now.

What is retained of apocalyptic eschatology is the incommensurability of the divine and the human—an "incoming" of that which is incommensurable with the proclamation concerning Christ. In this way, the prior linkage of

---

1. See Weiss, *Jesus' Proclamation*; Schweitzer, *Quest of the Historical Jesus*.

Introduction

Christian eschatology and the project of Western civilization was broken.

But this incoming of the eternal into time is addressed to the individual in what Kierkegaard called "inwardness."[2] Jesus and Paul's apocalyptic language describing the end of the old world and the coming of the new became something like an existential crisis. This old language, as Rudolf Bultmann suggested, had to be demythologized if it was to become usable today.[3] Christian existentialism, in its many guises, was born. And with it was born a distinction between eschatology and apocalyptic by which the latter gives name to a speculative world view of cosmic happenings.

There is no doubt that the first attempt to appropriate eschatological thinking was enormously fruitful for theology. But this eschatology had veered away from the drama of human history. This was understandable, given the ways in which connections to history ran into obstacles like the liberal project, or worse, the subsequent apocalypse of the Nazi project of a totalitarian political theology. But the call and claim of an apocalyptic consciousness embedded in the founding texts of Christian reflection could not be confined within the closet of the eternal now.

In 1960, another New Testament scholar, Ernst Käsemann, re-opened the issue of primitive Christian apocalyptic, bringing into question the solution of his teacher, Rudolf Bultmann. Bultmann had written that cosmological statements in the New Testament were anthropological statements, that statements about God were statements about humanity and vice versa. Käsemann truculently maintained that he was the theologian of the vice versa.

Käsemann argued that the existential demythologizing of Pauline concepts and language could not do justice

2. Kierkegaard, "Subjective Truth, Inwardness," 189.
3. See Bultmann, *Jesus and the Word*.

Introduction

to the world-historical scope of Pauline hope. Käsemann published a series of very influential essays at this time, and young theologians like Wolfhart Pannenberg and Jürgen Moltmann took notice. This influence was enhanced by Gerhard von Rad's work on the history of Israel's theology as a theology of history, a history generated by promise and oriented toward hope of world-historical transformation.

There are important, indeed fundamental, differences between the theological projects of Pannenberg and Moltmann, but they hold in common the recovery of an apocalyptic horizon of hope as essential to Christian faith. This means that history is not confined to the narrow horizon of the in-breaking of the eternal into time in the hearing of the kerygma, but is oriented toward the consummation of history as the history of nations, of peoples, and the cosmos itself. The future, as the future of God, comes toward us from the end of history. It is not a projection from the present as a sort of cultural optimism, nor is it the object of planning and program. It is God who comes toward us, rather than our achieving the divine reign of God, but approaching as the consummation of history and cosmos, as God becoming all in all.

For Moltmann, the coming of God is first of all found in the history of promise that enters into the consciousness of the prophets and which is expressed in Jesus' preaching. This awakens hope and casts theological thinking as a thinking of hope. But hope that is true hope and not optimism lives in the contradiction of the promise in the history of human suffering—a suffering that is above all brought to expression in the cross of Jesus as the event of the crucified God.

The work of Moltmann, as well as of Johann Baptist Metz, Dorothee Söelle, and others of this orientation, took on a radical political edge in what was often called a political

Introduction

theology. This theology grew out of the Christian-Marxist dialogue of the late fifties and early sixties and was a precursor in many ways to the emergence of liberation theology in Latin America and to the thought of theologians like Cone and Herzog in the United States in the early seventies.

I want to emphasize this opening, or re-opening, toward something like a political theology. For this has become the subject of considerable discussion in the domain of post-Marxist thinking in Europe, especially as it centers on a number of themes in the earliest eschatological texts of our Christian tradition: those of Paul.

Baruch Spinoza, a heretical Jewish philosopher writing in Holland in 1670, introduced the modern notion of political theology. Spinoza wrote an intriguing book called the *Theological Political Treatise*, which many consider to be the founding document of a historical-critical approach to the Bible. It was a survey of biblical literature aimed at making room for the emergence of what might be termed the modern secular state. After considering Moses and the prophets, Spinoza turns to Paul as what he calls the most philosophical of the apostles. That is, as one who writes so as to convince thinking people of the truth of his perspective rather than simply appealing to authority or revelation to warrant his assertions. And it turns out to be Paul who, Spinoza insists, agrees with Spinoza's own views—or rather, his views agree with Paul's. Thus was born the question of political theology, together with its connection to the thinking of Paul.

Carl Schmitt took up the term again in 1922 in a short treatise called *Political Theology* in which he famously maintains that all important political concepts are secularized theological concepts, taking the notion of sovereignty as the key political concept

Introduction

In 1970, about fifty years after *Political Theology*, Schmitt, who had reconciled with the Catholic Church, wrote *Political Theology II* in response to Eric Peterson, who had written an essay on the question of political theology in the history of early Christianity criticizing Schmitt's idea of political theology. In Schmitt's response, the old political thinker, tarnished irreparably by his association with a Nazi past, praises a 1969 address by a young but increasingly famous theologian, Jürgen Moltmann. The title of that address was "Political Theology," and it was a preliminary work toward what would become Moltmann's *The Crucified God*. After expressing certain doubts about some of Moltmann's formulations concerning the crucifixion of Jesus, Schmitt writes: "Nevertheless Moltmann is right to emphasize the political meaning which the worship of a crucified God ineradicably contains and which cannot be sublated into the 'purely theological.'"[4]

This is an absolutely decisive point: that a theology of the cross is necessarily a political theology. This is something on which the former National Socialist political philosopher Carl Schmitt, the great Jewish intellectual Jacob Taubes, and the post-Marxist theologian Jürgen Moltmann would all agree.

It is clear that a theology of the cross has long been deprived of any political meaning. Yet here we find it is political theology at heart. Churchly talk of the cross has become utterly innocuous from a political point of view. The most obvious fact of the cross—that it is, the execution of a subversive by the military regime of the Roman Empire—has been obscured by the theological fog of so-called atonement theories. It has been rendered both innocuous and unintelligible by talk of sacrifice for sin or forensic atonement and the like.

4. Schmitt, *Political Theology*, 150.

Introduction

It is in Paul, above all, that we see the emphasis of the messiah on the cross as the center of the proclamation. Paul writes: "I decided to know nothing among you but Jesus the messiah, and him crucified" (1 Cor 2:2).

Moreover, it is the message concerning the cross that shows the power of God entering the world so as to make it whole. Paul writes: "For the message about the cross is foolishness to those who are perishing but to us who are being saved it is the power of God" (1 Cor 1:18). And who are they who are "perishing"? Paul tells us it is "the rulers of this age who are doomed to perish" (1 Cor 2:6).

Jacob Taubes, in his book *The Political Theology of Paul*, asserts that Paul's theology is a declaration of war on Caesar. Taubes had noticed that Paul also says that this messiah was crucified by "the rulers of this age" (1 Cor 2:8), a reference to the Roman imperial regime. These are precisely the powers that Paul says are perishing; they are coming to an end. And what is it that brings them to their end? What is the self-destruction of imperial power? It is the cross itself, and the ongoing effect of the cross in the proclamation concerning the cross.

What could this possibly mean? Of course the cross is first of all a crisis for the proclamation of Jesus concerning the coming of God's reign. For in the face of that proclamation the empire demonstrates its power, its resolve, its capacity for "shock and awe." Jesus is executed as all rebels against imperial rule are executed; he is nailed to a cross, just as hundreds had been executed a century earlier in Corinth, to demonstrate that resistance is futile.

It is here that the resurrection of the crucified comes as the announcement of the impending collapse of Roman rule. If the power of empire is enforced by the fear of death, a fear that is shown to be futile in the resurrection of the

Introduction

executed, then the rule of fear, the threat of violence, loses all force. The rulers of this age executed the messiah, and in so doing, destroyed themselves.

This entails that a political theology is not to be established on the basis of the sovereignty of God—a sovereignty taken in hand by surrogates for God in empire and nation—but rather that political theology is to be rethought on the basis of the weakness of God, the folly or futility of God, even the death of God.

Although Carl Schmitt argued that the basic concepts of political thinking are secularized theological concepts, it makes a great deal of difference which theological concepts are secularized as political concepts. What emerges from a theology of the cross is a politics of the messianic.

We recall that Johannes Weiss had noted that the proclamation of Jesus had to do with the impending collapse of this world under the pressure of the coming of God, implying no continuity between or development from the old to the new. The relation is one of collapse, destruction, and catastrophe. Moreover, it is impending, imminent, and incoming.

Paul's thought is that the end of the ages, the end of the old world, has already come upon us in the message concerning the executed messiah. Concretely, this means that the old order currently represented by the empire of Rome has been dealt a fatal blow. We live in the time of the apocalypse. All that remains is the return of the executed, the full manifestation, or shining forth, of the messianic. We live in the interim, or what Giorgio Agamben calls in his post-Marxist political study of Paul by the same name, *The Time that Remains*.

This time, what Paul also calls the now time or *kairos*, is messianic time. To live in this time is to live in the end

Introduction

time, the time of the end, or as Agamben says, the time that time takes to end.[5]

The end—the collapse of history as the history of domination has come upon us, the in- breaking of the new as life and wholeness—has appeared ahead of time in the resurrection of the executed. But how is this "political?"

This answer becomes clear when we consider Paul's development of the basic theme of the thinking of the political: the theme of justice. Since Plato and Aristotle, the basic category of the political, or of what would be called political philosophy, is the theme of justice: the central theme of works like Plato's *Republic* or Aristotle's *Politics*. The question of the political is how social life is to be organized in such a way as to instantiate, to promote, and reflect justice, a question generally thought to concern the creation of just laws to govern society. Thus, there is an intimate association between law and justice. Indeed it was on this account that Hellenistic Jewish thinkers could suggest that the law of Moses would be the best way of bringing about justice.

We have then, in Paul's day, two competing ways of thinking about law and justice, both as law inspired, organized, and enforced as justice. There is Roman law as imposing justice upon an unruly world, and there is Mosaic justice in the law of Moses.

Paul agrees that justice is the fundamental issue for humans living together. It is the inexorable claim and call of God. The absence of justice means the collapse of the social historical order. God destroys, as Paul learned from the prophets, in the absence of justice.

The problem, however, is that law cannot itself bring justice. The law that intends justice all too often brings injustice. For Paul, this perhaps comes to a crisis in the lawful rejection and execution of God's own messiah. To the

5. Agamben, *Time That Remains*, 69.

Introduction

extent to which Paul is a representative of the law, whether of Moses as a Pharisee, or of Rome as a citizen, then he could not but be, as he says, "a persecutor" of those who adhere to this outlaw or criminal messiah.

But what if God, who requires, justice has overthrown the verdict of law and proclaimed the executed one to be just? Does God renounce justice? That is impossible, for God is nothing if not justice itself. What then? Justice comes apart from or outside the law. This is the astonishing claim of a messianic politics: that justice is necessary, but that it comes not from the law, but outside it, often from that which the law condemns.

In this sense, Friedrich Nietzsche was right both in seeing the centrality of the execution of the messiah by the law for Paul and in seeing that this awakens a Pauline project which can only aim at the destruction of the Roman Empire and its civilization.[6] Nietzsche was right about that, but he was also horrified. He took his stand with the values of Roman rule, the aristocratic values of the ruling elites. Nietzsche saw all this far more clearly than Christians who had forgotten entirely what the cross might mean in reality and saw only that Paul was concerned with issues of law and justice.

Paul's entire career as an apostle or delegate of the messiah is the creation of just societies as vanguards of the coming justice. Not individuals, but groups of sharing (*koinonia*), communes, assemblies that abolish categories essential to the world of domination: neither male nor female, neither Greek nor Jew, neither slave nor free. This is what Alain Badiou, the radical Marxist philosopher, calls the foundation of universalism.[7]

---

6. See Nietzsche, *On the Genealogy of Morals* and *Ecce Homo*.

7. Badiou, *Saint Paul*, 107.

Introduction

In this way, the messianic invades the old. It is not that the old evolves into the new, but rather that it is invaded by the new, a new that is its end, its abolition.

I have referenced Marxism and post-Marxism a few times already, and it is perhaps time that I offer a more overt explanation of the connection between Marxism and the appropriation of apocalyptic or even messianic thinking. The early theologians of crisis who appropriated the apocalyptic preaching of Jesus—Barth and the early Tillich and the early Niebuhr, for example—were also ardent socialists. Barth organized the miners of his parish to struggle against the depredations of capital. Tillich also organized workers to abolish capitalism, and in 1933 was the first non-Jewish professor to be dismissed by the Nazi regime after he wrote *The Socialist Decision*. And the young pastor Reinhold Niebuhr organized workers to strike against the capitalist Henry Ford. The rise of Stalin and the Second World War and the anticommunist crusade of a McCarthyite would change much of that.

But the worldwide student and worker revolution of 1968 would give fresh impetus to a reconsideration of Marx, now purged of Leninist and especially Stalinist perversions. And this is the climate in which Moltmann's embrace of a political theology can be understood, as well as the development of a neo-Marxist critique of capitalism in Latin American liberation theology.

Many reacted to the events of 1968 with deep misgivings, such as Pannenberg or Joseph Ratzinger (who would become Pope Benedict), but others like Moltmann and European intellectuals including Derrida and Badiou and Agamben rekindled a yearning for the coming of justice in a world dominated by structures of unjust exploitation and violence.

Introduction

This yearning for many around the world had been associated with Marx and Engels. They diagnosed the particular evils of emergent capitalism, with its degradation of the masses, its exploitation of earth and labor, and its headlong embrace of avarice and of imperial violence in support of avarice. They had sought to awaken the exploited proletariat to the arrival of a new age, then called democratic socialism. The old age was doomed by its own contradictions, making way for the coming of a new age, a new humanity, and a new justice. They called upon the exploited to organize themselves into cells or communes to prepare for the struggle to come and for the arrival of a future worthy of human dignity.

Writing in 1894, not long after Marx's death, Engels, Marx's constant companion and collaborator, wrote a history of primitive Christianity. In this and related texts, Engels develops an analogy between early Christianity and the workers' movement that he and Marx had so tirelessly cultivated.

But the analogy only goes so far. Engels thought the problem with Christianity was that it had to employ religious language to mobilize the masses against the empire. He also maintained that this religious language entailed a turning away from the troubles of this world to "heaven." In this he may be wrong, at least in regard to the language of Jesus and Paul. But Marxism itself may have made an even more fatal error, for in order to hasten the eschatological day, it embraced (with Lenin) a justification of violence and a strategy to seize the state as an instrument of coercion. The dream was turned into the nightmare of a totalitarian twin of National Socialism, a reign of terror that exceeded the French revolution, and a surrender to the apparatuses of control and management that abolished the political.

Introduction

What reawakened the dream? The civil rights movement led by Dr. Martin Luther King Jr., who in turn had been deeply influenced by Gandhi, played a significant role. Theirs was a vision of radical social transformation brought about by the powerless and the despised through the moral force of their own vulnerability, their own courage, and their own vision of justice as members of a beloved community.

That revolution did not always succeed. But it awakened a dream, a dream that was at once Marxist (or post-Marxist) and messianic. It was visible in the Sandinista revolt against the US imperial imposition of dictatorship, and in the protesters, armed only with candles, who brought the velvet revolution to Czechoslovakia and to Georgia, and in the end of dictatorship in East Germany and Romania. The dream was also glimpsed in Tiananmen, and on the green armbands in Tehran, and in the multitudes in Tahrir Square.

But the most radical text of messianic politics is still to be found in the writings of Paul, to which so many of today's most radical and committed intellectuals turn. They don't go there to find religion or seek instruction about God or church. They go there to find the testament of a new messianic politics that is capable of replacing the dying order of global capitalist depravity.

One more point I need to explain is already anticipated in the reference to Dr. King. Messianic politics has to come to terms with the temptations of what we may call messianism. This is the temptation to take control of the reins of history by force. For there is the messianism of Bush and bin Laden, and many other messianisms as well, that leave in their wake countless victims sacrificed to the

Introduction

coming of freedom and democracy, to the end of tyranny or capitalism, or even the great Satan of American imperialism. How to avoid the temptations of a messianic politics without relinquishing the hope for a radical transformation in history? Something like this question has inspired Jacques Derrida to write of a messianicity without messianism in his book *Specters of Marx*, which is concerned with how it is possible to inherit Marx and to find hope in that insistence upon the coming of justice.[8]

But even earlier, in passages reminiscent of Paul, Derrida had written of a weak messianic force, or a force of weakness that escapes the reign of violence and brings it to an end. For Paul had also spoken of the weakness and folly of the cross as that which demonstrates true divine wisdom or power. Not the power of the death penalty or the threat of war, but the power to promise life. In this sense, a messianic politics worthy of the name is a politics that is, as Jesus warned, "not of this world" (Rom 12:2b). That is, a messianic politics is not a simple replacement of one set of coercive empires by another. It does not play by the rules of what passes for the political, with its notions of sovereignty and violence, of law, and the friend-enemy distinction. It is another politics altogether. But it is a politics all the same: one that embraces justice not from above, but from below; not by killing, but by dying if need be; not by erecting institutions that command the heights, but by embracing the lowest, by a downward social mobility, by unrestricted welcome and generosity.

Philosopher Gilles Deleuze introduced a helpful distinction between what he called the arboreal (tree-like) structures and rhizomatic, (crabgrass-like) structure of historical movements.[9] This notion has been adopted as a

8. See also Naas, *Derrida from Now On*, 84.
9. Deleuze and Guattari, *A Thousand Plateaus*, 6–7.

xxvii

Introduction

political theory in Hardt and Negri's monumental trilogy, *Empire*, *Multitude*, and *Common Wealth*, which discuss the end of the capitalist militarist global regime and movements that herald a new polity, a new justice, and a new and effective generosity and solidarity. It is, perhaps, a messianic politics.

In order to have a sense of what such a politics might look like, we would do well to attend to the words of the master of messianic politics, the messiah himself. We are told that Jesus shared a parable; it is among the smallest of his parables, a sort of seed, since it follows the parable of the sower who went out to sow. This is the parable:

> What is the reign of God like and what could we compare it to? It is like a grain of mustard which, when it is sown on the earth, being smaller than all the seeds of the earth; but when it is sown, it comes up and becomes greater than all the herbs and makes large branches so that the birds of the air are able to dwell in its shade. (Mark 4:30–32)

Usually called the parable of the mustard seed, it is found in Jesus' sermon on the beach, which includes the parable of the sower. The sermon as a whole has to do with the mission of the reign of God. It is found in different versions in both Mark and Matthew. There is a considerable difference between the two versions, but in addition to the parable of the sower, they both include the parable of the mustard seed.

Jesus says: "Listen, take heed what you hear" (Mark 4:9). What did we hear?

The contrast between the smallness of the seed and the magnificence of the result is sometimes related to the way in which the seed of faith takes hold in the heart to grow by degrees into maturity and holiness of life. Or it is understood as the way in which the sowing of the seed of

Introduction

the gospel begins to bear results in the growth of a congregation so that it becomes a strong and vital church. But this has nothing to do with Jesus' messianic parable of the reign of God. The parable has to do with the mission of announcing the reign of God, a mission already launched by Jesus, a mission to be carried on by his followers. As Jesus says, listen.

The meaning of the parable is concentrated in a line that is really a kind of chorus or tag line Jesus' hearers and Mark's and Matthew's readers are expected to know. The line is: "The birds of the air make nests in its branches." It is a refrain that we know from a number of Hebrew Bible texts.

These texts begin with the image found in many cultures of the great tree at the center of the earth. This image had been used by Babylon in an imperial design illustrating the unification of disparate nations and peoples of the earth into a single great empire where peace and prosperity reign. The prophet Ezekiel, writing in Babylon, was among the first to use this image of empire, the great tree in which the birds of the air found rest, to speak of world political events from the perspective of Israel's faith. In the thirty-first chapter he addresses himself to the other great super-power of his time, Egypt. Egypt was growing great and arrogant, and so Ezekiel reminds Egypt of another super-power of old, the Assyrian empire that had fallen into decay. He does this in order to warn Egypt of a similar fate awaiting its own imperial and colonial designs. He writes:

> Who are you like in your gardens? Consider Assyria, a cedar of Lebanon with fair branches and forest shade and of great height, its top among the clouds. *All the birds of the air make their nests in its branches.* Under its boughs all the animals

Introduction

of the field give birth to their young. . . (Ezek 31:2–3, 6, emphasis mine)

The great tree is the mighty empire. And the birds that find shelter in its branches are the nations that find refuge, protection, and prosperity within the bounds of empire. Here it is the empire of Assyria, which in its pride was cast down: "On the mountains and in all the valleys its branches have fallen and its boughs lie broken in all the water courses of the land; and all the peoples of the earth went away from its shade and left it" (v. 12). And so, the prophet warns, will it also be for the great Egyptian empire: "Now you shall be brought down with the trees of Eden to the world below; you shall lie with the uncircumcised, with those who are killed by the sword. This is Pharaoh and all his horde says the Lord God" (v. 18).

This image of a great tree is found again in the book of Daniel. Here we find it in the dream of the great king of Babylon, the emperor Nebuchadnezzar:

> Upon my bed, this is what I saw; there was a tree at the center of the earth and its height was great. The tree grew great and strong, its top reached to heaven, and it was visible to the ends of the earth. Its foliage was beautiful, its fruit abundant, and it provided food for all. The animals of the field found shade under it, *the birds of the air nested in its branches*, and from it all living beings were fed. (Dan 4:10–12, emphasis mine)

When Daniel is summoned to interpret the dream, we discover that the great tree whose branches shelter the birds of the air represents Nebuchadnezzar and his great empire that stretches "to the ends of the earth" (Dan 4:34). We also learn that this great tree will be chopped down and the birds of the air will flee its branches, for in its arrogance the

Introduction

great empire had forgotten that true sovereignty over the earth and its nations belongs to the "Most High." Thus, the emperor is warned to "break off your sins by doing justice, and your iniquities by showing mercy to the oppressed" (Dan 4:27). We should not forget this address to the empire to do justice and show mercy to the oppressed. Only in this way can the empire survive the judgment of God.

Both in Ezekiel and in Daniel we find the judgment on the great empires of Assyria and Egypt and Babylon. There is not only judgment here, but also admiration for the security and prosperity that these great empires foster, if only for a time. The problem is that the great empires do not truly know God. And so they are avaricious, violent, and arrogant. They do not know the way of justice and true peace. They oppress the poor and destroy the weak. And so the great trees of empire must be cut down.

It need not always be so. For the prophets also dream of an empire in which peace and justice and generosity will rule in place of that violence and avarice and arrogance.

Ezekiel dreams of the coming of such an empire. In Ezekiel 17, the prophet speaks:

> Thus says the Lord God: I myself will take a sprig from the lofty top of a cedar; I will set it out. I will break off a tender one from the topmost of its young twigs; I myself will plant it on a high and lofty mountain. On the mountain height of Israel I will plant it, in order that it may produce boughs and bear fruit, and become a noble cedar. *Under it every kind of bird will live; in the shade of its branches will nest winged creatures of every kind.* All the trees of the field shall know that I am the Lord. I bring low the high tree; I make high the low tree; I dry up the green tree and make the dry tree flourish. I the Lord have

Introduction

> spoken it, I will accomplish it. (17:22–4, emphasis mine)

According to Ezekiel's vision, the great empire will come. But this empire reverses the values of worldly empire, the lowly are raised up and the proud brought low. And so true justice prevails and the nations of the earth nest in peace.

Is this only a dream? Can such an empire of justice and authentic peace ever come to be? Ezekiel is not alone in this dream. For in the Psalms we encounter this image again in the great hymn to creation of the Psalm 104. It begins, "Bless the Lord, O my soul. O Lord my God, you are very great; you are clothed with splendor and majesty, wrapped in light as with a garment" (Ps 104:1–2). Next, it speaks of the wonders of the created world:

> You set the earth on its foundations so that it will never be shaken. You cover it with the deep as with a garment; the waters stood above the mountains. At your rebuke they flee. You make springs gush forth in the valleys; they flow between the hills giving drink to every wild animal. The trees of the Lord are watered abundantly, the cedars of Lebanon that he planted, *in them the birds build their nests.* O Lord, how manifold are your works! In wisdom you have made them all. May the glory of the Lord endure forever. (vv. 5–7, 10, 11, 16, 17, 24, 31)

This long and beautiful hymn of praise will conclude with "Bless the Lord, O my soul." But immediately preceding that we hear, "Let sinners be consumed from the earth and the wicked be no more" (v. 35).

Why this odd and discordant note? It is to help us to realize that the earth described by the psalmist is the creation already cleansed of evil. It is creation restored and renewed, set free from avarice and violence. It is in this creation that the great trees put forth their branches and the birds of the air build their nests in them. It is in this renewed creation that the peoples of the earth at last find justice and joy. It is the new creation in which the violent stain of empire has been eradicated by the judgment of God upon all injustice and arrogance.

The image of the great tree in which the birds of the air find shelter expresses one of humanity's greatest hopes. It is the hope for the empire in which violence and avarice and arrogance will be expelled, the empire in which justice for the poor and vulnerable will reign, in which the peace of people living in harmony with one another and with nature will prevail. This dream is the secret hope that drives the course of human history. It is the yearning at the heart of humanity.

As Second Peter says, "it is the hope for the new heavens and the new earth in which justice is at home" (3:13).

This is the messianic hope crystallized in the image of the great shrub, herb, or weed in which the birds of the air find shelter, for this is the reign of God. That is why, in introducing the image, Jesus appears to underscore it so strongly. What is God's reign like? To what shall we compare it?

It seems that this empire of unrestricted love grows from the tiniest of seeds, from the announcement and enactment of the good news of God's favor. But notice: it is not a tree, it is an herb, even a weed, it is not an arboreal structure; it is more like crabgrass. In this, the messianic is radically different from the great trees of empire.

This proclamation does not promise that only a few individuals may be saved. Nor does it have as its goal that the church should grow into a powerful or influential institution. Rather, the aim and goal of the gospel is that the

Introduction

rule of the arrogant may be replaced by the companionship of the lowly, that the dominion of violence and hostility will be swept away by the peace that flows from justice, that wounded bodies and the wounded earth itself may be purged of violation and violence and made whole and clean.

This is the sort of eschatology that opens the space for the ecclesial praxis envisioned in Mukdani's work.

>   Theodore W. Jennings Jr.
>   Professor of Biblical and Constructive Theology
>   The Chicago Theological Seminary

1

Situating Ecclesial Praxis Today

> It is not enough to try to get back to the people in that past out of which they have already emerged; rather we must join them in that fluctuating movement which they are just giving shape to, and which, as soon as it has started, will be the signal for everything to be called into question. Let there be no mistake about it; it is to this zone of marked instability where the people dwell that we must come.
>
> —Franz Fanon[1]

FANON UNDERLINES THAT TODAY'S history should fix identity in some distant vanishing point and attend to its emergent figures rather than seeking "a past out of which they have already emerged." In other words, history is not merely the narrativization of events, but also the means by which the voices of those who were silenced and made invisible are heard. By moving across this zone, the historical subjects shift from one condition to another, crossing

1. Fanon, "On National Culture," 182–83.

An/Other Praxis

borders from space to space. Fanon's "zone of marked instability" is a borderline in the sense that it is always engaged as a historical moment of liberating praxis, as a new way of doing theology that will re(dis-)cover so-called "subaltern," or those subordinated others.

Praxis is described as a combination of reflection and action that realizes the historicity of human persons. It is the way people, especially the subaltern, respond to the social, economic, and political oppressions experienced in the present day. More closely, praxis includes what contemporary scholars term "perfomative acts," or the political discourses of understanding the world, changing it, and therefore liberating it. Thus, this type of action-reflection can open new spaces for subaltern people and affirm oppositional politics that reassess the value of self-determination and mutual solidarity.[2]

Today, the subaltern should no longer be explained as a "matter of non-believers" needing to be converted into a particular religious group. That is no longer the issue in this twenty-first century. Rather, it is a matter of the nonperson. The non-person is among "the human beings who are not considered human by the present social order—the exploited class, marginalized ethnic groups, and despised cultures."[3] Gutiérrez states it clearly in the context of Latin America, saying,

> The main challenge does not come from the nonbeliever but from the nonhuman—that is, the human being who is not recognized as such by the prevailing social order. These are the poor and exploited people, the ones who are systematically and legally despoiled of their being human, those who scarcely know what a human

2. Giroux, "Performative Politics," 5–23.
3. Grenz and Olson, *Twentieth-Century Theology*, 215.

Situating Ecclesial Praxis Today

> being might be. These nonhumans do not call into question our religious world so much as they call into question our economic, social, political, and cultural world. Their challenge impels us toward an evolutionary transformation of the very basis of what is now a dehumanizing society. The question, then, is no longer how we are to speak about God in a world come of age; it is rather how to proclaim him Father in a world that is not human and what the implications might be of telling non-humans that they are children of God.[4]

The non-person's situation—for example, poverty—is not due to only one type of oppression. Instead, there is always an interrelatedness of different structures of oppression (political, social, economic, racial, or sexual). This argument suggests that no liberation theology can fight just one oppressive force. Feminist theologians, for example, do not work only against sexism. Instead, they must struggle against racism, classism, and colonialism as related structures of women's exploitation and oppression.[5]

Thinking towards God's new creations in human history is a crucial element of theological struggles, and this liberating praxis serves not only as a discourse of critique and possibility, but also suggests possible directions for theology in the context of diversity. Such thinking relies upon the conviction that a new theological or cultural paradigm—a new synthesis of values—can or will probably emerge in any situation. It asserts that new knowledge will enable the subaltern to create new space, as well as a

---

4. Gutiérrez, "Liberation Praxis," x.

5. See, for example, Fulkerson, *Changing the Subject*; Izasi-Diaz, *Mujerista Theology*; Ruether and Skinner, *Women and Religion in America*; Russell, *Church in the Round*; and Chopp, "Latin American Liberation Theology."

transformative framework to understand God's praxis more creatively in the world.

However, this new way of doing theology needs to be injected into existing theologies. There are two historical reasons that support its importance. First, the liberation of underdeveloped countries from foreign dominations, which occurred almost everywhere immediately after the Second World War, has fueled the search for a collective identity with expectations for the formation of new free persons in a new society. In this post-colonial era, many people began to feel that they had been deeply affected in their identity, personhood, and understanding of life. Second, the reactions of indigenous peoples to Western imperialism, which were already visible in the beginning of the twentieth century, have brought forth renewed reflections on indigenous religious and cultural heritages.

Particularly, Christianity in Third World countries has felt impulses for renewal from a variety of sources. For example, as a consequence of independence from colonial rule, there has been a fundamental shift in theology in Christian churches calling for an attempt to reassess religious heritages introduced by Western missionaries. Rather than being solely subject to Judeo-Christian tradition, indigenous peoples want to find traces of God's work in their own history, and thus they design new theologies from within their own experience and knowledge. They want to understand themselves as mediators, witnesses, or messengers of an indigenous experience of God. For this reason, theology is articulated in a language that reflects the

Situating Ecclesial Praxis Today

concrete situations of exclusion and suppression of indigenous cultures and that works out strategies of liberation that correspond with traditional solutions. Thus, constructive critiques against Christian praxis have been at stake in the midst of a historically changed world.

Since the middle of twentieth century, liberation theologies[6] have become extraordinary works showing how the gospel is good news for the marginalized. Liberation theology sometimes refers to black theology, feminist theology, or various Asian and African theological developments, all of which later turned out to be manifold and complex and have since taken up new challenges. For in light of changing political, social, and church conditions in the past decades, liberation theologies have developed steadily as they face new challenges, take up new social subjects, and confront new questions. For example, many liberation theologians have been working toward a theology of witness in the actual context of contemporary post-colonial life. It is a kind of theology that is always in dialogue with tradition, contemporary thought, and existing ideologies throughout the world. This kind of contextual theology is closely bound to the search for Christian identity in the context of national liberation from colonial domination and to ecclesiastical liberation from the dominance of Western missions.

In order to witness, liberating theology requires a praxis that is especially lived and expressed in the life of community. This community of faith is said to become an expression of the presence of the kin-dom of God. In fact,

---

6. See Gutiérrez, *Theology of Liberation*; Boff, *Theology and Praxis*; Cone, *Black Theology of Liberation*; Ruether and Skinner, *Women and Religion in America*; Izasi-Diaz, *Mujerista Theology*. See also more recent works including Althaus-Reid, "Liberation Theology to Indecent Theology"; Goizueta, "Knowing the God of the Poor"; Hopkins, "More Than Ever"; Maldonado-Torrez, "Liberation Theology"; Petrella, *Future of Liberation Theology*.

An/Other Praxis

this conviction is shared by ecclesial communities that follow a pattern of Christian praxis based on commitments to stand in solidarity with the marginalized, in whose faces God is simultaneously hidden and revealed. From this faith-based community context, liberation theologians call upon the church to be the ecclesia of freedom. The ecclesia of freedom is a new corporeal life that makes peoples more free to be for and with the Other and with the whole humanity under God. To create this new life, liberation theology offers new theological reflections that help deconstruct unhealthy relations between theology and praxis. These reflections are at the root of the theological crisis of modern theologies that have impacted those who are the marginalized.[7]

Thus, a contextual theology of witness, that uses the ecclesia of freedom as its starting point, is not merely a discipline whose principal focus is the discovery, refinement, and articulation of timeless truths. Rather, it is preeminently concerned with praxis or practical involvement in specific situations of oppression. The praxis that brings liberation is the pathway to knowledge of God. From this particular point of view, God is not simply revealed in Scripture, but also in and through the praxis of the church to the extent that the church struggles on behalf of the oppressed. In this way, praxis becomes the criterion of truth. Truth is found in concrete actions—not theological abstractions—that serve to transform society and liberate the oppressed.

---

7. In this point, Peter Hodgson's notion of the "ecclesia of freedom" can be restated as a way to address this problem. See Hodgson, *Revisioning the Church*.

Situating Ecclesial Praxis Today

UNFINISHED WORK IN DOING ECCLESIAL PRAXIS TODAY

Many liberation theologians are in agreement that only within this set of practices and relations do theologians have access to intellectual and moral contexts whose interpretive sense and intelligibility inform theological discourses. Nevertheless, there have remained from the outset theological reflections on the commitment to liberate the marginalized, which are increasingly exercised by the marginalized themselves. Within this practical configuration, the oppressed gain a way of being and acting in the world, namely, a performative grasp of a field of possibilities that embodies a radically different story about creation and the place of human beings within it.

In the twenty-first century, ecclesial praxis towards the formation of new free persons has remained *deadlocked*; therefore, it is problematic. One of the reasons for this lack of progress is that the church tacitly relies on the modern conception of politics, and with it the practices, relations, images, and conversations that comprise what Max Weber calls the "iron cage" of liberal capitalist society.[8] Particularly, the model of triumphant Christianity has strongly impacted the "missionary" churches in Third World countries. It is a fact that the "missionary" churches still exercise disproportionate influence, spreading the religious faith of colonial masters, including belief in humanism, the use of grand narratives, and even projections of teleological utopia.

---

8. The iron cage refers to the increased rationalization of social life, particularly in Western capitalist cultures. Weber's iron cage traps individuals in systems based on technical, administrative, and market contingencies that control by rational calculation. See Weber, *Protestant Ethic*. Related to my arguments on the reliance on the modern praxis, see Boff, *Theology and Praxis*, chs. 1, 6, and 12.

An/Other Praxis

In her critique of modernity within her broader criticism of colonialism, Kwok Pui-lan points out that missionaries transported the debate between modernity and fundamentalism to Asia.[9] This debate contested what was true and what was nominal for Christian belief, thereby introducing concepts of doctrinal exclusiveness. The adoption of Christianity according to these modern understandings therefore meant acceptance of this narrowly exclusive, Western interpretation of doctrines and Scripture, which conflicted with more inclusive Asian cultures. The majority of missionaries in Asia were ethnocentric, believing both Western culture and Christianity to be superior to what they saw as less developed Eastern culture and religions. As a result of this ethnocentrism, it was assumed that Christianity could best be studied or adopted through Western philosophy and languages.

This condition has been brought about, not only through symbolic and cultural mechanisms, but also through a desire on the part of the colonized to imitate the culture of neocolonialism.[10] The politics of dominant Christian hegemony that originated from this liberal capitalism has largely gone unchallenged in determining both what is at stake for the church and what possibilities are open to Christians in a world of religious pluralism. Meanwhile, standard or grand narrative in religious historiography is still a colonial discourse in the sense that it silences voices and covers memories of whole groups.

This type of canon, or monolithic hegemony of the Western patriarchal church, has caused the Christian community to lose its eschatological power to shape believers' worldview, particularly the power to offer perspectives of

---

9. Pui-lan, "Sources and Resources," 25.

10. Franz Fanon's book *Black Skin, White Masks*, is helpful in understanding this condition.

the oppressed as historical and theological agents. This relationship between theology and praxis primarily perpetuates the modern assumption that religious faith is a private and essentially emotive type of consciousness, with no intrinsic (historical and social) relationship to the concerns and celebrations that make up everyday life. The ecclesial language currently used by Christian churches makes no reference to a relationship with the wider social order, or to any historical context. Moreover, the issues of transformation seem to be described as a natural process that has more to do with continuity than with the power tensions stemming from a diversity of social, political, and cultural issues.

Meanwhile, the apparent revisions exhibited by this canon have not yet challenged the subject matter or the paradigm of interpretations used. The constructions of this standard narrative have not been open to the development of a critique of the colonial enterprises. On the contrary, they have followed the path of traditional modern historical discourses, through which the past cannot be entirely seen as it really happened, since the grand narrative upon which they were based proved to be the only form of discourse, excluding all other perspectives.

In this standard narrative, the missionary ecclesial traditions are the central aspects through which everything is interpreted. Consequently, the superiority of these traditions, which is part of the construction of the West, was established through this dominant discourse. This discourse became characteristically universal such that every other particularity has to be explained through the dominant discourse to acquire any kind of validity. The canon of missionary religious traditions, as traditional historical discourses, can thus be characterized as an impetus of continuity, since the canon supports the ideas of progress and the superiority of the West over those in periphery, the indigenous. In this way, a colonial imagery, which is an explanatory model of what might be happening in the mind, was established, leaving the indigenous outside.[11]

This is the traditional arrangement that keeps indigenous Christians on the borderlands of society, either directly or indirectly. Consequently, the church cannot help them, and as Stanley Hauerwas contends, becomes "a life-style enclave and/or an umbrella institution where people are giving us the opportunity to associate with other people with their similar interests . . . that are not in any way shaped by Christian convictions."[12]

While facing the existing reality, the churches want to serve practices and goals that determine possibilities for everyday life within society. It then invests itself in an analogous process of making "normal" religious people who fit into the present order of things, confining itself to this process of normalization. It feels at home in the present social orders, and only perceives the need to tinker with its basic social connections. Only a handful of techniques remain to tinker with the dominant tendencies of pluralistic thought and practice. This signals an inability to articulate what is involved in the reconfiguration of the church's fundamental way of being in and acting in the world.

While they are still strongly affected by modern and colonial ways, churches face fresh challenges from the invasion of new forms of imperialism and colonialism that have begun to show their aftereffects, namely, as violations of old life patterns and understandings. Neocolonialism

---

11. The following books are helpful in better understanding the modern colonial system: Dussel, "Beyond Eurocentrism"; Mignolo, *Darker Side of the Renaissance*; Mignolo, *Local Histories/Global Designs*; Munslow, *Routledge Companion to Historical Studies*; White, *Content of the Form*.

12. Hauerwas, *After Christendom?* 93–96.

Situating Ecclesial Praxis Today

has taken a new form in the globalization of markets and capitals. Frederic Jameson has suggested that postmodernity has been the cultural logic of a new stage of capitalist accumulation and commodification that accompanies the formation of the world market.[13]

Such neocolonial conditions have ushered a different set of problems concerning identity into the twenty-first century. Its influence is not wielded through force and coercion, as with past colonial powers, but rather through the power of seduction, persuasion, and the production of desire as promoted through the Western mass media. As a result, many indigenous peoples begin to feel that the neocolonial powers have deeply affected in their identity, personhood, and understanding of life. For example, women are often torn between stereotypical images of the past constructed by traditional indigenous forms of patriarchy and Western images of the ideal woman of the future. In its contact with the East, Western Christian thought posited the non-Western as the essence of the Other. Since women and men were defined by Western constructions, colonization enforced an essentialized difference between Westerners and non-Westerners that objectified colonized people and constructed them as appendages to Western history.[14]

In response to the identity crisis (e.g., women) as influenced by neocolonialism, many critical responses (including theology) to this concern are preoccupied with analyzing difference and with challenging the reductionist binary constructions of class, race, and gender. Pui-lan argues that hegemony separates the colonizer from the colonized by superimposing an irreconcilable essence of differences while not acknowledging the diversity of social construction. This is an "ideological construction of

13. Jameson, *Postmodernism*.
14. Ibid.

An/Other Praxis

sameness and difference [that does not] . . . respect diversity in terms of race, gender, class, culture, and religion."[15] However, scholarly analysis of the emerging new empire-building and its cultural politics has direct implications for theological discussions about human liberation today.

From this postmodernist stance, liberation theology, especially in its early Latin American form, has been criticized as outdated and as having failed to provide adequate analysis of new structures of economic power. Liberation theology shares many features of modernist thinking, including beliefs in humanism, the use of grand narratives, and projections of a teleological utopia, the articulation of which does not challenge imperial rule.[16]

Meanwhile, such prominent issues as "liberation" and "the preferential option for the poor" remain static and, thus, unchallenged. Their inclusion in the narrative has been for the sole purpose of reinforcing the dominant identity and controlling marginalized peoples. Although this dominant discourse has given way to revisions, the better part of those revisions came from within the same dominant discourse. Therefore these projects of revision varied, but none opened up the field enough to allow voices from the outside to talk back to the center. When outside voices of were allowed to come in, it was not on their own terms. The dominant voices controlled the definitions, terms, and subject matter of the discourse. As John Pemberton asserts, religious discourse in particular created an image of the subaltern "Javanese," delineated by land of origin, race, and culture, which produced a picture that is fundamentally fixed and externally determined.[17]

15. Ibid., 79.

16. Compare this criticism with Hardt and Negri, *Empire*, 142.

17. Pemberton, "Disorienting Culturalist Assumptions," 119–46. See also Hefner, "Of Faith and Commitment," 99–125.

Situating Ecclesial Praxis Today

NEW CHALLENGES FOR ECCLESIAL PRAXIS TODAY

Taking this concern seriously, I suggest that churches work more seriously to promote a relevant ecclesial praxis that engages postmodernity in new ways and generates new insights for theological, social, political and economic thinking. This book addresses multiple struggles coming from borderlands that are searching for a constructive ecclesial praxis or an/other praxis.

Inspired by cross-cultural experiences and interdisciplinary studies in the areas of theology, ethics, and human sciences, I begin by re-imagining the concept of the ecclesia of freedom raised by liberation theologies. As a new way of thinking, the ecclesia of freedom offers an eschatological vision of hope to the community of faith, especially to those who are at the margins. It demands an ecclesial praxis that addresses God's new creation in its relation to God's people, especially the creation of divine gestalts in the public sphere. This theological task can be accomplished only when ecclesial praxis adds something to humankind's capacity for community and the church's ability to envision itself whole. In this sense, community of faith would be a measure of the Spirit's work in human life.

Taking the spirit of this revised ecclesia of freedom, ecclesial praxis continues by partnering with those who are relegated to the margins. Here I argue that the primary responsibility of ecclesial praxis today is to re(dis-)cover the subaltern, or the subordinated others. Here, the inclusion of the subaltern is necessary not only in searching out new impulses for theological practices, but also in bringing forth unheard voices from the margins to contribute fresh ideas and new opportunities for life. I believe that this theological task requires not only piety, but also politics, as well as a style of reasoning within the community of faith that combines theology and praxis. For example, we can ask what it means in this era of religious pluralism for the church to acknowledge and embrace its "abnormality" in the present ordering of creation, and ask also how the church concretely realizes, within multiple religious contexts, its status as minority.

The last two chapters of this book are strongly influenced by social locations that have shaped me towards an "always becoming someone new" identity as a native of Indonesia, an Asian-American, a United Church of Christ (UCC) ordained pastor, and a theologian. Here, I examine ecclesial praxis within broader paradigms and consider intellectual border crossings to propose an/other praxis that is liberating and that takes contemporary discussions of religious pluralism seriously. At least two prominent issues must be discussed in order to develop a context for the proliferation of a revised ecclesial praxis and mark a new stage in debates over liberation theologies.

First is the recognition of multiplicity and diversity in contemporary cultures, lives, and thought as central characteristics of these times. This multiplicity of identity contributes to people's feelings of being "outsiders within" in their relationship to both Christian and non-Christian and communities, illustrating the complexity of the construction of national, religious, and cultural identities. It is from these margins that people approach the Bible, articulate their theology, nourish their faith, and connect with other Christians who also live at the margins. For example, this recognition is important to considerations of Christianity in Indonesia, where Christianity is one among several imported religions that have been influenced by Hinduism, Buddhism, and Islam. Like other religions, Christian beliefs have never completely eliminated traces of the indigenous religions of Indonesia. As Andreas Yewangoe explains, "*Tribal religions* are still alive in many parts of Asia. In many cases elements of these primordial religions are still found in the religious lives of the adherents of Islam and Christianity as well. For example in Java (Indonesia) the *Kejawen* (the Java Religion) still exercises influence."[18]

Second, we must also deal with the question of how Christianity engages with pluralism in its theological practice and thought. From here, Christians' recognition and appreciation of other cultural traditions, especially the voices of those have been oppressed in the history of Christianity, should significantly change ways of thinking about God's revelation to humankind and encourage a rethinking of inherited notions of mission in Third World countries. What is at stake here is new Christian thought and action in the struggles of national liberation from colonial domination and in ecclesiastical liberation from the dominance of "Western" missions.

Given this situation, it will not be enough for theological reflections to recognize the locality of a theological tradition; for example, the recognition of a European theological tradition that was accepted for centuries as normative for the church, as one of many theologies. This recognition would remain only partial without a critical evaluation of the negative impacts of the dominant theological tradition on other traditions. Instead, people no longer want to be subject solely to Judeo-Christian traditions. They also want to find traces of God's work in their own history and to design new theologies from within their own philosophy. The issue is finding new dogmatic formulations, dogmatics that are shaped from liberation experience instead of religious creed.

---

18. Yewangoe, *Theologia Crucis in Asia*, 19, emphasis in original. See also Yewangoe, *Theologia Crucis in Asia*, 222–42 for further detail.

An/Other Praxis

In this shift in theology, the question of how we think about God is fundamental to the whole way Christians see themselves and the worlds in which they dwell as God's creation. The affirmation of God's preferential option for people at the margins of society not only signals that God's justice is characterized by a partiality toward the oppressed, but also that God works from the margins of the dominant socio-cultural matrix, choosing to use these margins as salvivic agents. In this context of ecclesial freedom, God's characters should be oriented to what I will call subaltern, or subordinated others.

This implies that any form of ecclesial praxis that ignores the preferential option for the margins in favor of a more general orientation to otherness must implicitly support the exploitative interests of the early twentieth-century theologies. Such theologies are, I believe, irrelevant to the lives of today's Christians, in Indonesia particularly, and in Third World countries generally. The notion that God, in Jesus Christ, is revealed in a privileged, preferential way among the subaltern should be categorized as a challenge to established theological and ecclesial practices.[19] In other words, one cannot engage in Christian theology, or even think theologically, without confronting the claims implicit in the preferential option of the oppressed.

For this reason, Christian theology that takes the spirit of religious pluralism must seek to create social spaces that break down the tightening grasp of social division and hierarchy by building upon human solidarity. It is, I believe, an/other praxis that seeks to engage history with the intent of helping the powerless locate themselves within it. It constructs a decolonial imagery through which the borderlands becomes a discursive space from which history is written.

19. Gutiérrez, *Essential Writings*, 78–148.

2

Re-imagining Ecclesia of Freedom

> [The ecclesia of freedom] . . . describes a community of faith and struggle working to anticipate God's New Creation by becoming partners with those who are at the margins of church and society.
>
> —Letty M. Russell[1]

BASIC NATURES OF THE ECCLESIA OF FREEDOM

THE ECCLESIA OF FREEDOM refers to an ecclesiological notion that stems from the practical need to define Christian identity. It is the Spirit's work in a community of faith that helps people's struggles to be partners with those who are at margins of the church and society. The term ecclesia (from the Greek *ekklesia*) has a different meaning from traditional

1. Russell, *Church in the Round*, 39.

ecclesiology, which fosters the cultural captivity of the church and leads it away from its prophetic role in human history. Instead, it refers to an emerging church that would be non-hierarchical, participatory, and inclusive, and one whose community members would engage in liberating praxis and live out an ecumenical mission.[2] It places its emphasis "more upon the public than the private, the social than the individual, liberation than liberty, equality than hierarchy, inquiry than authority, praxis than theory, the ecumenical than the provincial, the plural than the monolithic, the global than the national, the ecological than the anthropological."[3]

This new emphasis implies that the church should be referenced as an indecipherable entity because there is no such thing as "the church" per se, but rather individual churches. The self-understandings of marginalized Christian communities have come into awareness that when they gather, they are gathering as church. They do not consider themselves as parts or pieces of a larger entity we call the church as truly ecclesial expressions.

This sense of being a church represents an ecclesial freedom that is built from the paradigm of Jesus, whose ministry was inclusive, liberating, suffering, and impelled by the Spirit of life. Taking the notion of freedom drawn from literature arising out of liberation theologies, Hodgson describes Jesus as "the radically free person" who proclaimed and enacted a gospel of liberation from internal

---

2. Peter Hodgson sees these new ecclesial visions emerging in marginalized communities as a sign of "ecclesial wholeness beyond all patriarchy, all clericalism, all misogynism; in communities of the black church as a paradigm beyond all racial prejudice; and in the Latin American base communities as a paradigm beyond all class oppression" (Hodgson, *Revisioning the Church*, 12).

3. Ibid., 17.

Re-imagining Ecclesia of Freedom

and external forms of bondage.[4] Moreover, this Jesus, it is believed, has been raised from the dead and is now at work in the world actualizing the freedom he once engendered. His resurrection is the energizing force in dialectics of emancipation and redemption by which liberation historically occurs. Under this reasoning, the real meaning of freedom is neither autonomy nor membership in a privileged group, but an openness to the liberating power of God with others, which engenders new and transformative understandings of subjectivity and community. This transformation is consummated by the vision of a coming true communion of free subjects, namely the kin-dom of freedom proclaimed by Jesus as the reign of God and the true destiny of humankind.[5]

THE PROMISES OF ECCLESIA OF FREEDOM

Ecclesia of freedom provides a vision of Christian hope, not just hope in the next life, but also hope in this life—not just individual hope, but also communal hope. This new vision of ecclesia makes eschatological hope inseparable from the matter of "ends" for human reality.[6] It also serves as a basis for articulating an ecclesial praxis that provides the community of faith with both a perspective of the future and a guiding light toward a meaningful life in the present. It serves to answer people's troubles and questions in the present day as well as for the coming reign of God. The com-

---

4. Hodgson, *New Birth of Freedom*, xiv.
5. Ibid.; Boff, *Church: Charism and Power*.
6. Compare with Moltmann, *Theology of Hope*, 134. In this book, the separation between the term "end" from the notion of "hope" is understood in his critique of modern theologies. In his current works on systematic theology, the terms "end" and "hope" seem clearly inseparable from one to another.

munity is empowered to identify itself as a *counter-society* in the sense of an alternative community with "counter-cultural consciousness," to put it in Walter Brueggemann's terms.[7] The community of faith will, in turn, be able to extend its current possibilities to a more relevant and contextual theological praxis.

This vision of ecclesia is politico-eschatological because it urges Christian communities to relate this doctrine of hope to understandings of humanity, value systems, and worldviews. The language of ecclesia would be relevant in making reference to relationships within the wider social order and historical realities. The issue of social change or transformation would be revealed as a historical process that has more to do with power tensions articulated around a diversity of social, political, and cultural issues than as only a natural process of continuity.

Ignoring this renewed effort, communities of faith will lose the power to shape believers' worldview or conduct. Christian communities will also be less able to energize people through thoughtful consideration of a Christian hope that embraces, as Jürgen Moltmann explains, the object hoped for and the hope it inspires.[8] It means that Christianity will lose its ability to imagine a new future in the midst of cultural change, religious plurality, and globalized oppression of the marginalized.

Counter-historical Discourses around Ecclesia of Freedom

Liberation theologies have offered ecclesia of freedom as a new way of thinking about the church to thematize its

---

7. Brueggemann, *Prophetic Imagination*, 21.
8. Moltmann, *Coming of God*, x–xvi.

Re-imagining Ecclesia of Freedom

liberating praxis. This kind of thinking is controversial because it strongly emphasizes a counter-historical discourse that confronts and challenges contemporary theology. As Peter Hodgson describes it,

> Contemporary theology . . . [deals with] the issues related to the conflict between traditionalists and (post)modernists, the prospect of a rebirth of the church in the Latin American base communities [liberation theologies] . . . the impact of religious pluralism, and to the current crises in ministry . . . attempting to work out a comprehensive theological understanding of the ecclesial community in light of these controversies—a vision of ecclesia that might function as both a critical and a productive paradigm in the life of actual churches.[9]

By taking the ecclesia of freedom seriously as both a critical and productive paradigm, liberation theologians challenge the monolithic hegemony of patriarchal churches[10] and argue that it is foundational for the marginalized Christian communities. Marginalized communities situated in ecclesial freedom are historical and theological agents imbued with revolutionary activity and the prophetic role of the church called by God. These communities of faith always gather around the memory of Jesus, who had given God's life for the excluded and the disinherited.[11] In this way, only when such a realization of the Spirit's work is made does the true meaning of the church come more

---

9. Hodgson, *Revisioning the Church*, 9.

10. Ibid., 13–19. The five crises Hodgson lists are cognitive, historical, political, socioeconomic, and religious.

11. Gutiérrez, *Theology of Liberation*, ch. 6.

An/Other Praxis

resolutely into view. This recognition is important to Hodgson's notion of the ecclesia of freedom.[12]

According to Hodgson, ecclesia of freedom identifies itself as the Spirit's work in not only inspiring the life of the church, but also orienting itself toward God's eschatological new creation. The gathering of the people of God is grounded in the coming of the kin-dom of God.

However, this eschatological character demands ecclesiological reflections that do not immediately begin with the church itself, but rather with God's new creation in relation to God's people.[13] For example, Leonardo Boff argues that focusing on this eschatological character is crucial for the new way of thinking about the church because the church no longer characterizes itself as "incarnational," the church which takes Jesus Christ as the model for understanding itself as the whole.[14]

According to the doctrine of incarnation, God, in one of the modes of God's triune being, was once and for all made human in the person of Jesus Christ. Just as Jesus Christ achieved salvation for all people, the church must prolong that mission throughout the centuries. This incarnational model of the church is seen as exclusive because it has failed to take into account the decisive event of the resurrection. Boff explains, "[After His resurrection,] the body of spiritual Christ can no longer be considered as a physically definable entity from which we can deduce the limits of the church, the body of Christ . . . the church must

---

12. Hodgson, *Winds of the Spirit*, 276–316. Cf. Moltmann, *Church in the Power*, 289; Moltmann, *Source of Life*, 92–96.

13. Ibid.

14. Boff, *Church: Charism and Power*, 144; see also Hebblethwaite, "Incarnation," 256–60.

Re-imagining Ecclesia of Freedom

be thought of in terms of the risen Christ, identified with the Spirit."[15]

In contrast, Boff proposes a bottom-up model that finds its ecclesiological roots in the term "ecclesiogenesis," which is the notion of the "base communities" as a process by which the church takes its form in a highly situated and predominantly pre-institutional sense.[16]

In his observation on this conception of ecclesiogenetic thinking, Lewis Mudge argues that the formation of each local faith community should be a social-linguistic process empowered by the Spirit and articulated metaphorically by the whole content of Scripture. Mudge uses this reasoning to support his claim that it is possible to think in social scientific ways about the formation of such ecclesial spaces.

Mudge explains that Christian communities of faith are lived expressive embodiments of the people-configuring work of the Holy Spirit within the social and cultural worlds in which the churches exist.[17] Christian communities can discern their Spirit-formed social realities in the world and bring them into a divine frame of reference that makes them visible. The ecclesia of freedom thereby articulates human communities around them as spaces in which the Spirit's people-gathering power is active. By proclaiming the gospel, by celebrating the liturgy, and by acting prophetically, they signify that God is continually forming communities of people to be agents of justice, peace, and freedom.

The most significant point here is the affirmation that the ecclesia of freedom is adequately understood as a gathering of people who bring with them all kinds of

15. Boff, *Church: Charism and Power*, 145.
16. Boff, *Ecclesiogenesis*, 59.
17. Mudge, *Sense of a People*, 89–115.

An/Other Praxis

life-substance.[18] Such life-substance may come in many forms, whether creativity, generosity, or bravery, but finds purpose in community life. That is, a community that aims to represent the identity of Jesus Christ and thereby to articulate the shapes of God's presence in the world through the work of the Holy Spirit. In this way, the interpretation of the world as the space of God's reign involves Hodgson's "phenomenology of spirit," which traces the formation of meaning as the Spirit does its work in shaping human life.[19] The community members experience the Spirit at work in them through the signs generated by their effort to exist and desire to be. By taking form in this world of social meanings, "this trans-signification of social reality would bring a sense of real presence to the ever continuing dialectic of power and imagination."[20] This interpretation implies that the church both expresses its freedom by participating in deeper symbolic reality and also opens itself to wider and emergent symbolic worlds. It is the real meaning of freedom, which includes both inner receptivity to the liberating power of God and openness to a wider world that makes a congregation an entity with particular commitment.

THE HISTORICAL GOD AS THE HORIZON (NOT CAUSE) OF MEANING

The ecclesia of freedom becomes an inclusive inquiry that encourages a theology of God and history that is radical in its political thrust and human consequences. To develop this conception of God and history in complex mutual interconnection with one another, Hodgson employs

18. Ibid.
19. See Hodgson, *God in History*; Hodgson, *Winds of the Spirit*.
20. Mudge, *Rethinking the Beloved Community*, 22.

Re-imagining Ecclesia of Freedom

Hegelian concepts and insights, particularly his Trinitarian theology.[21]

Trinity is foundational for Hegel (and, it seems, for Hodgson) because it offers one of the most sophisticated critiques of the monarchical position that insists on the non-relationality of the divine and history. Unlike Hegel's contemporary, Friedrich Schleiermacher, who proposed an essentially "absolute dependence" to the problems modernity posed for the Christian understanding of God's relation to humanity and the world, Hegel radicalized Christian thinking about God's "mighty acts" in history. Hegel replaced the traditional idea of an utterly transcendent God, acting on the world from the "outside," with a new Trinitarian conception of God's involvement in the historical process that constitutes both the world and human existence.

Hodgson makes a strong case for Hegel as an important resource, for his reconstruction of a theology of history not only eschews an ironic response to history, but also provides at least an adequate theology of history that would avoid triumphalistic or pessimistic (tragic) extremes. Drawing on Hegel's work, Hodgson develops an illuminating conception of God-and-history in complex mutual interconnection, a conception that enables him to draw both themes together into a coherent synthesis from a wide range of contemporary voices. These voices particularly come from liberationist convictions that insist all forms of oppression and totalitarianism must be resisted and overcome.

Hodgson believes that only by critiquing the classical position of God, as rooted in the legacy of Schleiermacher,

21. Hodgson, *God in History*, 51–112. See also Hegel, *Philosophy of Religion*, 3:84, 87; Hegel, *Phenomenology of the Spirit*; Troeltsch, *Christian Faith*; Troeltsch, *Theology and Religion*.

An/Other Praxis

can we enter into a new phase of history, one that will be filled with both unprecedented possibilities and enormous dangers. This is the vision that pervades his works on constructive theology, which think through the intrinsic relationality of the divine and history, as well as their mutual interaction in the self-actualization of the divine and the historical.

According to Hodgson, God and history should be seen as correlative, co-constitutive categories. God is self-actualized in and through historical process, and history is shaped by what he terms "gestalt,"[22] which transcends it. God is effectively present in the world, not as an individual agent performing observable acts, nor as a uniform inspiration or lure, nor as an abstract ideal. God is therefore not the cause of meaning; rather, God is the horizon of meaning. God is present in specific shapes or patterns of praxis that have a configuring, transformative power within historical process.

The notion of a shape, or gestalt, connotes something dynamic, specific, and structuring, but it avoids potentially misleading personifications of God's action.[23] The idea of gestalt, Hodgson believes, is fundamental to understanding God's real presence in history. He writes:

> History is a process of victories and defeats, of configurations and deconfigurations; yet it is empowered and lured onward by a transfiguring practical ideal, a gestalt of freedom, the image

---

22. In his discussion of God, Hodgson refers to the concept of gestalt. Hodgson finds the notion of gestalt first in Hegel's *Philosophy of Religion*, where it refers to the historical configuration of the "divine idea" in the form of an "objective spirit." He finds it again in Troeltsch's notion of *Gestaltung*, or the forming of "historical individuals" in the sense of coherent configurations of historical factors. See Hodgson, *God in History*, 194.

23. Hodgson, *God in History*, 205.

Re-imagining Ecclesia of Freedom

> of a communion of solidarity, love, mutuality of recognition, and undistorted communication. The gestalt that lures and empowers history is the gestalt of God. It appears as such when the historical field has been cleared of all pretensions, of all autonomously based projects and powers, and when human projects and powers are seen rather to be the bearers, the vehicles of God's presence, of God's strange empowering kind of power.[24]

This gestalt of loving freedom, which is the very figure of God, must take shape in concrete historical praxis. Otherwise, it would remain an abstract ideal. There is no triumphal march of God in history, no special history of salvation, only a plurality of partial, fragmentary, ambiguous histories of freedom.

In ascribing personhood to God, Hodgson begins with a Hegelian account of the immanent Trinity, whose personhood is constituted by relational acts of love and freedom, and who exist in three modes of being.[25] He asserts that "God becomes truly and fully God, God as Spirit, only through the world."[26] Thus, Hodgson affirms that the world plays a significant part in the divine life.

In this way, Hodgson dismisses Karl Barth's position of abstract God-in-history's attributes of perfection as essentially untenable in the light of "postmodern temper."[27] He argues that Barth needs to admit that if "God is so immanent in the world as to be 'the being of its being,' then the world must be immanent in God."[28] Hodgson's position

24. Ibid., 193.
25. Ibid., 152.
26. Ibid., 156, 164.
27. Ibid., 97. See Barth, *Epistle to the Romans*.
28. Ibid., 109.

here seeks to affirm that God is internally related to the world and the world is internally related to God.[29]

In this way, the historical process may be understood as a dialectic between two interacting factors: the ideal and real, the possible and actual, the universal and particular, the transcendent and immanent, the divine and human. What is important here is not a distinction between planes, one superhistorical and the other historical, but a single plane—the fabric of history—that is made up of many distinctive, interwoven threads.[30] Hodgson's specific strategy is to look for the gestalt of freedom in scattered, fragmented forms in, with, and under the manifest structures of society. This theological move from theoretical constructs into a focus on praxis parallels this move from the "divine idea" in German idealism to the notion of historical forming or shaping.

Nevertheless, Hodgson expresses his thinking surrounding gestalt in a variety of ways. Here is an example: "God is present in specific shapes . . . This is what I mean by the divine *gestalt*."[31] Yet, it is not easy to see this divine configuration in history. It requires a serious engagement with Hegel's work. Hodgson clarifies that to speak of God is to speak not of a person, but of a gestalt, or shape, that embodies both the person and the work of Jesus Christ.[32] However, after the death of this divine figure, the divine gestalt takes on "a new, communal identity, a sociohistorical dynamic that coalesced in and around a specific human being and with which the human being is still identified."[33] In this way, personality of Jesus is "not lost but taken up into a higher

29. Ibid., 96.
30. Hodgson, *Winds of the Spirit*, 193–95.
31. Hodgson, *God in History*, 205.
32. Ibid., 234.
33. Ibid., 209.

Re-imagining Ecclesia of Freedom

unity or structure"[34] that is found within the life and work of the people and the church. For this reason, Hodgson suggests that divine gestalts are best seen by communities of faith involved in the search for a truly public realm for practical reasoning in the human interest. Thus, the ecclesia of freedom deals not only with the nature of the church in the new paradigm, but also with its forms for action.

THE CREATION OF GESTALTS IN PUBLIC SPHERES

The ecclesia of freedom should become a context in which mutual obligation, as justice, is expressed in historical forms and actions. It demands that the community of faith contribute to humankind's capacity to envision itself whole. In Boff's perspective, ecclesial communities that take actual people into account, as well as their myriad connections to worlds beyond their churches' borders, require a large measure of sociological realism.[35]

Only by adding to humankind's capacity can ecclesial praxis make possible struggles for God's new creation in its relation to God's people through the search for gestalts in the public sphere. They are the divine gestalts, the shapes of "love in freedom," the shapes given form by "certain images associated with the ministry and the death of Jesus, images of compassionate freedom and liberating love."[36] God is present in the historical now, opening the way for a real future, yet grasped only in struggles to realize that future.

34. Ibid., 271–73.

35. Mudge uses sociological realism to establish his means of synthesizing sociological resources with a revisionist Reformed theology committed to the struggle for human liberation and global conversation. For a detailed explanation, see Mudge, *Sense of a People*, ch. 2.

36. Ibid., 195.

An/Other Praxis

Hence, every ecclesial community is responsible to provide the world with communicative languages and symbols that keep the question of God open.

Specifically, it is a discourse concerned with the social space that makes language about God, and therefore faith itself, possible. That is, the faith is about what is theologically required to make and keep life human as it grows out of historical experience, especially the experience of liberation. The ecclesial freedom of speech is based not on the self-understandings and needs of ecclesiastical institutions, but rather on the character of God's humanity in the process of being gathered. The ecclesial community, as the ongoing embodiment of the "Christ Gestalt," is significantly called to act in ways that clarify the communal shape, or the gestalts, revealing what God has done in the ecclesial community beyond visible ecclesiastical boundaries.[37]

Human praxis and the history of freedom, beyond their historical value, have intrinsic value for humanity.[38] Interestingly, Hodgson extends the notion of gestalt beyond the boundaries of Christendom by looking for the gestalts of freedom in the public spheres. It is possible, however, that it may have been his intention for these "shapes of freedom" to extend and embrace the whole cosmos. In such a context, human struggles can be perceived affecting the nature of the consummation of history in God.

Ecclesial communities take the role of a "transfigured mode of human community" founded on the life, death, and resurrection of Christ, created by the power of God as Spirit. It is the Spirit of God who works among the people. In this sense, the ecclesial community can be a measure of the Spirit's work in human life. The ecclesia of freedom, as a new theology of church, can become a kind of critical social

37. Ibid.
38. Hodgson, *Winds of the Spirit*, 154, 315–16.

Re-imagining Ecclesia of Freedom

theory that can explain how the potential for human community is interpreted by being gathered into congregations. It moves through history, encountering and transforming lived meanings into configurations that form a theological picture of human reality through which men and women can realize their humanity through a renewed understanding of their relationships with each other and with their world.

The struggle of the ecclesial community thus becomes multiple struggles for humanity that go through a truth-testing process on the way to being finally ordered by the configurative power of the Spirit, whose identity we know in Jesus Christ. Therefore, the Christian responsibility is to work for the enhancement and expansion of freedom in order to integrate the various shapes of freedom into a more inclusive, multifaceted, wholesome matrix of communicative action and cultural practices. In this way, this process becomes a continuing transformation of the privileged and an ongoing liberation of the oppressed.[39]

But this theological realization of humanity does not happen all at once in any one time or place. It happens here and there in gestalts of freedom and hope, in moments that have been called "polis," or the reasoning toward ideal measures for achieving the good society.[40] Mudge correctly observes that although this ideal polis is only ever momentarily fulfilled, their understandings should not be taken for granted.[41] Such moments of the polis are among the gestalts whose description Hodgson derives from Hegel's thought and in whose reality he sees God's presence in history.

Finally, the radicality of Hodgson's God-in-history acknowledges that the interpretation of the world as the space

39. Ibid., 234.
40. Hodgson, *God in History*, 193.
41. Mudge, *Sense of a People*, 210.

An/Other Praxis

of God's reign involves a version of Hodgson's "phenomenology of spirit," which traces the formation of meaning through the Spirit's shaping and configuring work in human life.[42] In other words, it can offer the world a language for grasping its own present truths and future possibilities. The community members experience the Spirit at work in them through the signs generated by their effort to exist and desire to be.

---

42. Hodgson, *God in History*; Hodgson, *Winds of the Spirit*.

3

Naming the Subaltern

> [Praxis] is about the creation of a public sphere, one that brings people together in variety of sites to talk, exchange information, listen, feel their desires, and expand their capacities for joy, love, solidarity, and struggle.
>
> —Henry A. Giroux[1]

WHO IS THE SUBALTERN?

SINCE THE SIGNIFICANCE OF otherness in postmodern and postcolonial thought has confronted the ways Christians think about faith in many areas, it is possible to reconstruct what liberation theologians call "the option for the margins."[2] This reconstructed theology for and from the margins is not only necessary in searching out new impulses for theological practices, but also to extending voices

---

1. Giroux, *Disturbing Pleasures*, x.
2. Taylor, "Subalternity and Advocacy," 29.

An/Other Praxis

from the margin to contribute both fresh ideas and new opportunities for life.

The crisis of modernity has caused conversations of otherness and difference that refer to the relation of oppressor and oppressed, and not to the free flow of differences, and so has resulted in charitable projects that do not change the position of subordinated others. This unchanged situation raises significant challenges for the church's serious engagement in the "liberatory a priori" in order to create space for the voices of the subordinated others. Mark Taylor suggests the use of the term "subaltern" as an accurate expression of a liberatory a priori. He explains,

> The term ["subaltern"] will enable deeper reflections on the problems of advocacy and solidarity. The very linguistic construction of the term *subaltern* bears witness to the way it can critically engage the world of postmodernist discourse and is itself a part of that world. Clearly, the term signals an interest in otherness (difference, diversity, deferral in a flux of signification and location) by way of its major linguistic unit, "-altern" (from Latin *alter*, "other"). Nevertheless its prefix, "sub-," deepens and orients its interests in alterity to experiences of sub-ordination. To study the subaltern is to study the subordinated others, usually the others who have been subordinated because of their otherness.[3]

This notion of subaltern is important because it not only engages the postmodernist's interest in otherness, it also critically acknowledges a liberatory a priori that refuses to take subordination as simply one more mode of otherness. Instead, the term "subaltern" keeps theologians "concrete, specific, manifold, hybrid, fully pluralistic in ever

3. Ibid..

Naming the Subaltern

new ways, when speaking and acting in relation to experiences of subordination."[4] In this way, subordination must be considered in relation to alterity, and to its many other diverse forms and manifestations.

This state of new theological consciousness raises the question of what constitutes the de/colonial imagery for subordinated communities. I argue that it indicates a basic notion of the de/colonialized identity that should be deeply related to, and that the subaltern's performative acts against the dominant culture that Giroux describes can be an alternative. This counter-cultural discourse is opposed to the dominant discourse, which is fundamentally based upon essentialism and assumptions bound up with the western concept of modernity. This modern pattern of thought organizes itself according to exclusive categories of binary opposition: civilized/primitive, Christian/pagan, native/alien, white/black, male/female, and rich/poor. These identifying categories have supported a myriad of exclusive and oppressive practices.

Postcolonial theorist Edward Said describes this colonial identity as the "worst and most paradoxical gift" because it was "to allow people to believe" in these binaries, which any postcolonial discourse sees as a serious problem.[5] This modern colonial attitude was instrumental in fostering a distorted sense of self-identity for the colonized. Such a condition only leads the colonized into a state of self-division, for even while resisting the colonizer through the process of decolonization, they also possess a conscious desire to imitate the attitude and thought of the colonizer. The systemic demand for fixed identities and absolute differences is undermined by its own insistence on mimicry.

4. Ibid., 30.
5. Said, *Culture and Imperialism*, 336.

An/Other Praxis

A counter-cultural discourse is needed not only to expose these dominant discourses, but also to recover histories that can help people see and interpret their cultural past using their own lenses. Liberation theologies have shown that counter-cultural discourses can break down epistemological patterns of knowledge and experience by shifting the role of the people from objects of a dominant history to subjects of their own history.

While dominant discourses relegate people outside the center of power to the margins of the normative knowledge, counter-cultural discourse challenges the normative knowledge in bringing forth the voices of the subaltern. In this sense, many liberation theologians and other liberation scholars acknowledge that knowledge and experience must be understood through social construction, rather than through standpoint theory. This understanding places an emphasis upon the communal construction of knowledge and experience.[6]

This perspective calls for communities of faith to honor inclusivity, mutuality, and solidarity. A counter-cultural discourse demands that the foundationalism that has informed modern Western thought for so long be challenged to engage in new dialogues, and at the same time expands beyond the narratives that deny the existence of differences, which has promoted forms of infantilism and oppression.[7] Particularly, it calls theologians to a co-suffering with the subaltern, who are voiceless or even subordinated, as they struggle both to transcend and transform their disempowerment.[8] In this space, theologians must locate themselves on the side of the subaltern and not merely acknowledge subordination, but also celebrate resistance. This is a state

6. Pui-lan, *Asian Feminist Theology*, 39.
7. Giroux, *Disturbing Pleasure*, 155–56.
8. Chopp, *Praxis of Suffering*.

of liberation in which the subaltern know which of their wants are genuine because they finally know who they really are. In such a state of collective autonomy, they have the power to rationally and freely determine the nature and direction of their collective existence.

Such theologians also challenge Christian communities to model inclusive subaltern communities for the sake of the world. These newly conceived communities are not to remain isolated in their diversity, however. In order to have a global consciousness, diverse communities must also envision and work towards a wider community constituting the body of Christ.

Thus, plurality that these theologians celebrate does not undermine Christian unity, but rather enriches it with more genuine authenticity. In calling for partnership with the subaltern, they stress that the justice-seeking faith community must shift its theological orientation from ecclesial-centered to people-centered.[9] I believe that in pursuing this goal, an inclusive diversity in the subaltern communities will be recognized, and mutual responsibility will replace scapegoating and victimization. The interconnection of multiple oppressions and identities will also be recognized as a basis for the unity of global Christian communities amidst the diversity of local communities.

RE(DIS-)COVERING THE SUBALTERN

There have been several paradigmatic engagements to re(dis-)cover the subaltern within the writings of religious historiography shaped by a colonial enterprise that depended on a canon and standard narrative, which later developed into a grand narrative. There have also been various

---

9. For example, see Pui-lan, "Mission of God in Asia," 23.

An/Other Praxis

scholarly attempts to acknowledge the subaltern as historical subjects through struggles for liberation. However, these subaltern scholars have also created preconditions for the current questioning of universalizing claims. Particularly, many proposals from the outside have appeared as people from border groups keep writing their own stories and keep talking back to the center, not from within dominant discourse, but from its borderlands.

The issues surrounding this borderland have to open a discursive space in order to construct a decolonial imagery of the unheard voices of the subaltern community. In this social location, dialogue with other fields will serve as the key to bringing new voices and perspectives together. It is a discourse that does not seek its own validation from the center, but rather in the historical voice of people in the borderlands.[10] Thus, the idea of borderland is necessary to give a new meaning to history. In this sense, participants are engaged in a process of re(dis-)covery by unmasking the modern/colonial character of the dominant discourses.

Examining the borderland as a paradigm exposes colonial attitudes and gets to the roots of the ideology of manifest destiny. From this perspective, history is not seen as the narrativization of events, but rather as the means by which voices of those who were silenced are heard. The borderlands become discursive locations where these histories can be re(dis-)covered without the influence of normative discourses. Colonization, marginalization, and oppression are revealed in this space from the side of the suffering. In other words, these histories are not told to benefit the peoples in the center of power, but to liberate the peoples outside of it so that voices that dominant historical discourses had silenced for so long are re(dis-)covered. In addition, the borderlands, as discursive locations, become the space

10. See Anzaldúa, *Borderlands/La Frontera*.

Naming the Subaltern

where concepts, paradigms, and hermeneutical keys are deconstructed and reconstructed. This space is where history is seen through the eyes of the peoples subordinated from the historical narratives—people outside the dominant discourse.

One of the most important contributions scholars of subalterns have made is the recognition that the canon has to be deconstructed in order to be reconstructed. This realization sets aside previous models that divide into parties of the population, the homogenization of plurality, and racial/ethnic or gender paradigms that support subordination and perpetuation of standard narratives. This means that the openness to voices from outside has to come without any kind of controlling agenda.

Liberation theologies like feminism dramatically challenge hierarchies built on those binaries. This challenge is based upon the argument that Christianity has contained in its central doctrine the symbols of a divine/human hybrid[11] that mimics and transgresses the operative metaphysical binaries of imperial times. In this imperial situation, the human subject is seen as a hybrid event torn by the asymmetries of power. Liberating praxis can be placed in the framework of the continuing search for a new humanity that liberation theologies have seen as an essential driving force in liberation endeavors.

In respect to liberation theologians, Giroux acknowledges that the goal of fostering critical awareness of a liberating cultural action is a creative, fruitful effort toward a cultural revolution that is undertaken by the subaltern themselves.[12] The essential features of liberation theology's

---

11. The historical concept of hybridity has been produced by the indirect subjection that stimulates survivalist strategies of mimicry and appropriation.

12. Giroux, *Border Crossings*, 104.

An/Other Praxis

emerging human beings include the capacity to critically analyze the present, to fashion their human destiny, and to be oriented toward the future in hope. These new human beings, whose actions are directed toward a society yet to be built, are more of a motivating ideal than an already realized reality and generalized in full accord with both the spirit and the letter of the church's teaching.[13]

But inasmuch as these theologians are content with exalting a single, liberating identity such as the poor, blacks, or women, they remain more or less within the same problematic modern paradigm. Such criticisms are particularly true of the subaltern's voices and experiences, particularly those coming from the borders or Third World contexts that do not take part in theological discourse. In the case of "the Latino/a Americans,"[14] for an example, their subaltern voices are largely lost within the religious historiography of the United States because the colonial imagery has left this subordinated community without a historical voice, at the border of the historical discourses.

Another reason for their silence is that the prevailing paradigms such as the black/white paradigm and ethnic/racial pluralism perspectives ignore them.[15] This is why it can be argued that the winners, those in power, control standard narratives. Regarding this issue, scholars suggest that the best way to bring justice to all subaltern is to include a paradigm that focuses on the diversity issues of class, gender, and race or ethnicity. These issues must not be seen as individual topics, but rather as integrative issues in order to re(dis)-cover the suppressed, silenced voices of

13. Ibid., 213–14.

14. See Saldíva-Hull, *Feminism on the Border*, 59–160; Perez, *Decolonial Imaginary*, 55–74.

15. Saldíva-Hull, *Feminism on the Border*, 27–58; Ruether and Skinner, *Women and Religion in America*, 1–11.

Naming the Subaltern

the subaltern and achieve their liberation. It is also a way of creating ties between different subaltern groups to resist the oppressive character of the dominant discourses.

Giving voice to such people will change the geopolitics of knowledge. This means that integratively including racial and ethnic perspectives in discussions of class and gender issues opens discourses to new voices, places, stories, and relationships by breaking through established models.

Most critically, such deconstruction of the modern projects embedded in standard narratives would bring down colonial imaginaries which promote the idea that western missionary traditions serve as catalyst for religious histories in many of Third World countries. As an example, for indigenous Christians who live on the island of Java in Indonesia, this deconstructive effort would create a subaltern community in which decolonial indigenous imaginaries could be expressed in the integrative construction of a Christian Church and a harmonious society.

This, in turn, leads to a new paradigm that offers multiple identities for Javanese Christianity in Indonesia. First, we need to sort out who is the subaltern for Javanese community. However, there is also a need to dissolve the false identity of otherness into its real multiplicity and variety to build an account of the world as seen by the others, Javanese Christians—an account that can transform them into the center of discourse.

In doing this, Gayatri Spivak demands that her readers turn the "critical glance not specifically at the putative identity of the two poles of a binary opposition, but at the hidden ethico-political that drives the differentiation between the two."[16] This approach attends not only to the processes through which those limiting categories are created, but also to the between spaces in which they may

16. See Spivak, *Critique of Postcolonial Reason*, 332.

An/Other Praxis

be undermined. These in-between spaces, or interstices, are more than descriptive. They give rise to what Homi Bhabha calls an "interstitial perspective,"[17] that challenges conventional understandings of identity. This perspective accompanies a new sense of subjectivity that is resistant to the dynamics of subjection, an "interstitial subjectivity." Identity is not here a fixed set of traits, but rather something that evolves through a continuing process of interrelation, identification, and differentiation. Giroux ascribes this understanding of identity to border intellectuals who do not exist in simple, theoretically safe zones of identity. Their identities always change according to the complexities of never feeling at home. The concept of homelessness can mean a back-and-forth process towards an ever-becoming present and an ever-becoming possibility in terms of who we are.[18]

This perspective is necessary in ecclesial praxis today not only to overcome the problems caused by the "internal" decolonization discourses, but primarily to help the Christian subaltern claim their own identities in the midst of cultural and religious plurality. These identities are based on "shared colonial history, multiple religious traditions, rich and diverse cultures, immense suffering and poverty, a long history of patriarchal control, and present political struggles."[19]

As a form of counter-cultural discourses, ecclesial praxis exposes the Eurocentrism that is still at the center of the cultural life of the colonized. At the same time, it attempts to move the marginalized voices of the subaltern toward the center stage of history, not based upon a concept of universalism, including binarism, but due to differences

17. Bhabha, *Location of Culture*.
18. Giroux, *Living Dangerously*, 167–68.
19. Pui-lan, *Discovering the Bible*, 24.

Naming the Subaltern

in political orientation. This is not only to theorize the subaltern, but to understand the characteristics of subordinated identity that increase the discursive capacity to speak meaningfully within a more diverse community. In this way, ecclesial praxis may also help subalterns to appreciate the complexity of the diversity of the church.

Given this complex nature, ecclesial praxis that re(dis-)cover the subaltern would never simply celebrate differences. Rather, people who give voice to their own hopes and dreams in this border-crossing work understand that theories that celebrate hybridity or difference are in danger of collapsing into a "triumphalist self-declared hybrid."[20] Because such thinking recognizes hybridity as something that remains inalterable, there is, however, great potential for resistance.

Like postcolonial theory, ecclesial praxis always questions the "rules of recognition"[21] by which insider and outsider are identified. As a consequence, it threatens practices of exclusion and subordination that are based on those rules of recognition. Taking this into account, Giroux aligns himself with postcolonial theorists who suggest that the subaltern constantly negotiate individual positions (discursive borderlands) between contradictory realities, between a sense of belonging to certain groups and exclusion from others.[22] But in order to achieve this negotiation, Giroux suggests that the subaltern need to be border-crossers: people who are able to cross into different zones of cultural diversity to form what Trinh Minh-Ha calls "hybrid and

20. Spivak, *Critique of Postcolonial Reason*, 361.

21. Bhabha, *Location of Culture*, 110.

22. Giroux, *Border Crossings*, 18–20. Pui-lan, who finds hope in this "in-between" space, argues that the subaltern identity can be negotiated through cultural hybridity and different social locations (discursive boderlands). See Pui-lan, *Asian Feminist Theology*, 19.

An/Other Praxis

hyphenated identities."[23] In the next chapter's discussion of an/other praxis, I will explain in detail how border-crossers rethink the relationship of self to society, and of self to other, and how they may deepen the moral vision of the social order. Although this hybrid border-crosser position is seemingly painful, it can be an enriching position, nurtured by multiple sources.

Specifically, Kwok Pui-lan's work is particularly helpful in dealing with issues of liberation a priori that relate to cultural practices and reading strategies emerging in colonized societies. I find at least two insights from her work enrich the decolonial imagery construction of the subaltern.

First, Pui-lan notes that the dynamics of claiming multiple identities are contextualized within political engagement, but they are not concerned with a particular essence of gender or culture. She locates the essentialist debate within Greek metaphysics, universalizing colonialist discourse, and the present western controversy with language in relation to Asia. She goes on to define Asian woman with multilayered, fluid descriptions that are partial, situated, and context-bound. This allows her to retain gender, race, and culture as political categories without reverting to universalizing, objective discourse.[24] It also necessitates the weaving of various different narratives arising from multiple identities. She refers to Jean-François Lyotard's observation that as our roles shift in each narrative as the interaction of our shifting roles produces new meanings and alternate narratives.[25] She concludes that multiple subject positions produce multiple identities within multilevel discourses.[26]

---

23. Minh-Ha, *Woman, Native, Other*, 374.
24. Ibid., 25–26.
25. Ibid. See also Lyotard, *Postmodern Condition*.
26. Ibid., 38.

Naming the Subaltern

Second, while Pui-lan is careful to honor groups of people who are silenced and vulnerable, she takes issue with the epistemological privilege of the oppressed. She challenges the belief that Third World people, particularly subaltern such as the poor and the marginalized, have an a priori privilege in the biblical interpretation. This concept of epistemological privilege assumes that the subaltern include natives of the biblical texts, thereby increasing the ability of today's subaltern to understand and identify with these texts. Pui-lan suggests that such identification fails to appreciate the construction of the native, and overlooks the dissimilarities between the historical development of Palestinian societies and our own, assuming that only authentic natives can understand the Bible, and claiming a fundamental distinction between colonial and native societies.

These problems "commit the sin of Orientalism" by collapsing native into one category and ignoring the varied social and historical constructions of each society. They also perpetuate the sharp and false distinction between colonial and all other societies. Although colonial cultures constructed white supremacy, they are not "fundamentally different" from all others. This assumption only serves to strengthen the "we-they dichotomy that has given such power to the white people."[27]

The epistemological privilege of the oppressed also assumes that one is either the oppressed or the oppressor, without realizing that multiple identities create a mix of privilege and marginalization: "The Other is never a homogeneous group; there is always the Other within the Other."[28] Full appreciation of diversity from the subaltern can mean that we will need to move beyond this type of identification. As a result, Pui-lan proposes a model of dia-

27. Pui-lan, "Jesus/The Native," 82.
28. Pui-lan, "Post-Colonial Perspective," 78.

logical imagination that will engage the multiple identities of people and communities around the world with their multiplicity of biblical interpretations.

Here she consistently locates the "critical principle of interpretation" not in the Bible, but in the communities of men and women who are reading the Bible with dialogical imagination for their own liberation.[29] She suggests that a dialogical model of biblical interpretation will examine the multiplicity of interpretations that arise out of particular communities that in turn are differentiated by identities such as race, class, culture and sexual orientation. This dialogical model, which takes root in Mikhail Bakhtin's *The Dialogic Imagination*, listens to subordinated voices and insists that dialogue must take place not only among Christian communities, also but with human communities of all faiths.

Such dialogue will more accurately reflect the multiple identities of all people, particularly Asians who live in a multi-scriptural context. Instead of approaching biblical interpretation from a singular perspective, such as gender, race or class, Pui-lan insists that the intersections of multiple identities and contexts are crucial to a dialogical model that "emphasizes plurality of meanings, multiplicity of narratives, and a multi-axial framework of analysis."[30]

---

29. Pui-lan, *Discovering the Bible*, 19. See also Pui-lan, "Postcolonial Imagination," 29–51.

30. Ibid., 37–40.

4

Crossing Borders Intellectually

> [To cross borders is to] rename difference through the process of crossing over into cultural borders that offer narratives, languages, and experiences that provide a resource for rethinking the relationship between the center and margins of power as well as between themselves and others.
>
> —Henry A. Giroux[1]

TERRAINS OF AN/OTHER PRAXIS

REFIGURING ECCLESIAL PRAXIS WITHIN broader paradigms is a fundamental step in extending cultural politics of transformation into new spaces that empower subaltern to articulate their counter-cultural discourses. In taking this step, I will address the question of defining an/Other praxis within a border-crossing paradigm that not only

---

1. Giroux, *Resisting Difference*, 209.

An/Other Praxis

goes beyond reproductive approaches,[2] but also situates those practices within the field of cultural politics. Rather than moving pedagogy away from the dominant discourse of methods, counter-cultural discourses will continue to address wider social relations and power struggles. In this chapter, I will begin with mapping out pedagogical terrains of praxis as a discourse of critique and possibility that will connect radicality of Freirean liberatory pedagogy.

From Reproductive to Productive Paradigm

Historically, liberal educational discourses have discussed pedagogy as providing opportunities for individual improvement, social mobility, and economic and political betterment to marginalized sectors of society such as the poor and ethnic minorities.[3] This conception of education has been problematized by the emergence of critical reproduction theory that rejects the assumed neutral and apo-

---

2. Reproductive approach refers to texts and social practices whose messages, inscribed within specific historical settings and social contexts, function primarily to legitimate the interests of the dominant social order. Such a theoretical discourse focuses on how powers (material and ideological resources) are used to reproduce the new social relations and attitudes. It also addresses questions of experience and agency by emphasizing resistance and the capacity of individuals and groups to contest hegemonic control, creating new frameworks in which domination-resistance are apparent. Although reproductive discourse addresses *critical* resistance, it fails to provide a project of transformation. For this reason, Henry Giroux claims that border-crossing pedagogy is able to accomplish transformative projects. See Weiler, *Women Teaching for Change*, 14–18; Giroux, *Theory and Resistance*, 76–100.

3. These discourses have been very much disseminated through different kinds of educational programs within diverse countries. See Watson, *Education in the Third World*; Feibleman, *Education and Civilization*; Lazear, *Education in the Twenty-First Century*

Crossing Borders Intellectually

litical structure of educational institutions. Particularly, this critical theory points out that these academic institutions were social and cultural agencies and very much involved in the legitimation and reproduction of dominant material and ideological conditions.[4] The works of Henry Giroux and Stanley Aronowitz provide a critical discussion of the shortcomings and possibilities of three important theories within the reproduction paradigm of schooling that have had a major impact on contemporary educational theory and practice.

The first is the economic-reproductive model as discussed in the works of Louis Althusser and by scholars Samuel Bowles and Herbert Gintis.[5] These theorists analyzed the links between the economic structure of society and the transmission of certain skills and knowledges that determined social sectors in order to perpetuate the current system.

The second is the cultural-reproductive model as represented by the work of Pierre Bourdieu.[6] The central tenet of this perspective is analysis of the mediating role of culture in the reproduction of class societies, resulting in an empowering study of the dynamics of class, culture, and domination.

The final theory is the hegemonic-state reproductive model as represented by the works of Antonio Gramsci and later by Michael Apple.[7] Within this paradigm, analysis is

4. For an example of analysis on critical reproduction theory, see Giroux, "Theories of Reproduction," 257–93; Giroux, *Theory and Resistance*; Giroux and Aronowitz, *Education Under Siege*.

5. Giroux and Aronowitz, *Education Under Siege*, 74–79. See also Althusser, "Ideological State Apparatuses"; Bowles and Gintis, *Schooling in Capitalist America*.

6. Giroux and Aronowitz, *Education Under Siege*, 79–87. See also Bourdieu and Passeron, *Reproduction in Education*.

7. Giroux and Aronowitz, *Education Under Siege*, 87–95. See also

An/Other Praxis

centered on the complexity of the role of the state in the educational system, leading to diverse discussions about credentialism, access, expertise, and providing important categories to analyze content and form within the official distribution of knowledge.[8]

It can be said that critical reproduction theory represents a challenging alternative discourse to traditional educational theory. But by not addressing questions of experiences of powerlessness and agency, critical reproduction theory fails to provide alternatives to the reproduction of dominant systems and norms by not offering projects of transformation that move people from feelings of despair to concrete strategies of change according to an emancipatory vision.

Based upon this failure, resistance theory, which is a mode of discourse or perspective that takes the notion of emancipation as its guiding interest,[9] has emerged as an alternative discourse. Paulo Freire was among the educational theorists who developed an important critical analysis of resistance theory that emphasizes its empowering elements while also recognizing its limitations. Freire powerfully theorizes the phenomenon of internalized oppression and develops a brilliant strategy through his conceptualization of conscientization and problem-posing.[10]

But resistance theory that does not take oppression into account as part of the complex situation remains within the classical parameters of the economic structure.

Gramsci, *Selections from the Prison Notebooks*; Apple, *Ideology and Curriculum*.

8. Giroux and Aronowitz, *Education Under Siege*, 69–114.

9. Giroux, *Theory and Resistance*, 107–12.

10. See notable examples of Freire's oeuvre, which include *Pedagogy of the Oppressed*, *Education for Critical Consciousness*, and *Politics of Education*.

Crossing Borders Intellectually

Similarly, resistance theory limits itself to the analysis of acts of resistance by the powerless, without considering other behaviors that are less visible, which remains problematic.

Paulo Freire

Freire's liberatory pedagogical methods originally developed in the particular historical and political circumstances of postcolonialism in Brazil and later Chile and Guinea-Bissau.[11] His writings thus need to be understood in the context of the political and economic situation of the developing world. Freire conceived of oppression in class terms and viewed education in the context of working people's revolutionary struggles. Equally influential in Freire's pedagogy was the revolutionary role of liberation theology in Latin America. Like liberation theologians, Freire's personal knowledge of extreme poverty and suffering challenged his deeply felt Christian faith, grounded as it was in the ethical teachings of Jesus in the gospels. Freire's pedagogy is thus founded on a moral imperative to side with the oppressed that emerges from both his Christian faith and his experience of suffering in the society in which he grew up.

In his influential book, *Pedagogy of the Oppressed*, Freire presents the epistemological basis for his liberatory pedagogy and discusses the concepts of oppression, conscientization, and dialogue that are at the heart of his pedagogy.[12] Freire shows his concern for education as a means of promoting revolutionary action toward social and political change, arguing that education should be carried out by and with the oppressed and not for them. This argument is based upon an assumption that in order to be fully hu-

11. Perhaps the best introduction to Freire's pedagogical methods can be found in Freire, *Education for Critical Consciousness*.

12. Freire, *Pedagogy of the Oppressed*.

man, people must not be the object, but instead the subject of change. This seminal work thus entails conscientization of the oppressed. That is, it attempts to make people aware of their oppressive situation and show them that through their own creative participation, they can transform oppression. In Freire's pedagogical method, praxis is the word for uniquely human action. Praxis is defined as the action and reflection of people upon their world in order to transform it.[13]

Freire organizes his approach in terms of a dualism between the oppressed and the oppressors and between humanization and dehumanization. This organization between opposing forces reflects his own experiences doing literacy work with the poor in Brazil, a situation in which the lines between oppressor and oppressed were clear. For Freire, humanization is the goal of liberation; it has not yet been achieved, nor can it be achieved so long as oppressors continue to subjugate the oppressed. That is, liberation and humanization will not occur if the roles of oppressor and oppressed are simply reversed. If humanization is to be realized, new relationships among human beings must be created. As Freire explains,

> Because it is a distortion of being more fully human, sooner or later being less human leads the oppressed to struggle against those who made them so. In order for this struggle to have meaning, the oppressed must not, in seeking to regain their humanity (which is a way to create it), become in turn oppressors of the oppressors, but rather restorers of the humanity of both.[14]

---

13. Freire, *Practice of Freedom*, vii.
14. Freire, *Pedagogy of the Oppressed*, 44.

Crossing Borders Intellectually

Hence, the struggle against oppression leading to humanization is utopian and visionary. Freire says, "To be utopian is not to be merely idealistic or impractical but rather to engage in denunciation and annunciation."[15] By denunciation, Freire refers to the naming and analysis of existing structures of oppression; by annunciation, he means the creation of new forms of relationships and being in the world as a result of mutual struggle against oppression.

Thus Freire presents a theoretical justification for a critical pedagogy that aims to critique existing forms of oppression and to transform the world by creating new ways of being, or humanization. From this viewpoint, critical pedagogy is not a proposition to be assessed for its content, but is a part of a system of belief and praxis that affects the power structures of society. By promoting a critical consciousness of self and other, critical pedagogy seeks to foster a connected and interdependent sense of self that undermines separateness, hierarchy, and anthropocentrism. In so doing, critical pedagogy constitutes a social and cultural criticism that implies an analysis of deeply politicized aspects of educational institutions, policies, and practices that can and must be oriented towards social change.[16]

Many critical scholars of the 1980s used Freire's *Pedagogy of the Oppressed* as the theoretical justification for their work, especially his statement concerning the need for and possibility of change through "reading the world and the word," or cultural literacy as a means to empower silenced subjects.[17] The use of Freire's pedagogical method has empowered silenced subjects. Freirean pedagogy has helped many subordinated others to "name their reality" and

15. Freire, *Politics of Education*, 57.

16. See Giroux, *Pedagogy and the Politics of Hope*, 3–118. Cf. McLaren, *New Information Age*; Freire, *Pedagogy of the Oppressed.*

17. See Freire and Macedo, *Reading the World and the Word.*

An/Other Praxis

to gain a more global perspective of the structural forces that lead to their oppression. Armed with this perspective, subordinated people in grassroots religious communities and social movements have mobilized to transform reality. But when Freire's work is examined from the perspective of recent critical pedagogy,[18] certain problems emerge that reflect difficulties that have arisen when Freire's ideas are enacted in specific settings, for Freire set out his pedagogical goals of liberation and socio-political transformation as universal claims; his theory rested on a belief in transcendent and universal truth.

According to postmodernist pedagogical critics such as Peter McLaren, modern utopian thinking is always framed in terms of the Enlightenment's dream of progress and individual autonomy through the use of reason, or the Hegelian dialectical march of the "Geist" to self-identity, or the Marxist account of class struggle.[19] This thinking has created totalizing and teleological "grand narratives" that have silenced and excluded a multiplicity of voices in history. For McLaren, this drive towards totality resulted from the Enlightenment's elevation of rationality above all human faculties. Released from the bonds of tradition and nature, reason loses its initial critical and emancipatory aims and becomes, in the hands of an imperial subject, purely instrumental.[20]

Although postmodern[21] critics have not criticized Freire directly, their challenges against the modern proj-

---

18. I refer here to the works of Henry Giroux as well as other feminist educators who are particularly influenced by postmodernist thought and the writings of women of color.

19. McLaren, "Postmodernism and the Death of Politics," 193–215.

20. Ibid.

21. Following liberationist standpoints in critical pedagogy such

Crossing Borders Intellectually

ect of progress and knowledge problematize Freire's anthropology and social ontology, which borrowed heavily from the Hegelian-Marxist master narrative. Freire's liberating pedagogy can be seen as problematic within the postmodern context because it brings together the crisis of utopian thinking, which increases socio-cultural fragmentation by deepening and broadening capitalism. What is at stake here is the viability of resistance to oppression based on the exercise of critical consciousness, or conscientization,[22] a notion that lies at the heart of modern emancipatory projects of thinking and especially at the heart of liberation theology.

An additional problem is the abstract quality of terms such as humanization, which do not address the particular meanings imbued by men and women, black and white, and other groups. The assumption behind *Pedagogy of the Oppressed* is that in struggling against oppression, the oppressed will move toward true humanity. But this leaves unaddressed the forms of oppression experienced by different actors and the possibilities for struggles among people oppressed differently by different groups.

This assumption also presents humanization as a universal category, without considering the various definitions

---

as those of Giroux and McLaren, I mean the term "postmodernism" as not simply a style of thought that is skeptical of "grand narratives" or that gravitates around the plurality of particulars, alterity, difference, hybridity, and playfulness. Postmodernism is instead a cultural form that is related to the "rise of more flexible modes of capital accumulation, and a new round of 'time-space compression' in the organization of capitalism" (Harvey, *Condition of Postmodernity*, vii). Thus, the postmodern condition is basically a historical condition. See Jameson, *Postmodernism*; Eagleton, *Illusion of Postmodernism*.

22. "Conscientization" is an exercise in intra-historical transcendence, or "revolutionary futurity," as Freire puts it, as "beings in the process of becoming . . . unfinished, uncompleted beings in and with a likewise unfinished reality" (Freire, *Pedagogy of the Oppressed*, 84, 72).

this term may bring forth from people of different groups. For example, Freire speaks of the oppressed needing to fight the tendency to become "sub-oppressors."[23] This means that the oppressed can only be identified in the abstract as object, within one pattern of oppression.

Furthermore, the usage of the oppressed in this way raises difficulties in Freire's use of experience as the means of acquiring a radical literacy, of "reading the world and the word." At the heart of Freire's pedagogy is his insistence that all people are subjects and knowers of the world. Their political literacy will emerge from their reading of the world—that is, their own experience as subjects. This reading will lead to collective knowledge and action. Yet this assumes that when the oppressed perceive themselves in relation to the world, they will act together collectively to transform the world and move toward their own humanization. The nature of their perception of the world and their oppression is implicitly assumed to be uniform for all of the oppressed.

To call the universal and abstract claims of *Pedagogy of the Oppressed* into question is certainly not to argue that Freire's pedagogy should be rejected. Although critics have found it to have some serious shortcomings, the emancipatory impulse behind his liberating pedagogy is certainly worth preserving. To uphold this impulse, however, it is necessary to undertake a radical revision of Freire's pedagogical projects.

For this reason, I argue for a critical postmodern rereading of Freire that points to ways in which the project of Freirean pedagogy may be enriched and re-envisioned. Freire's ethical stance in terms of praxis, and his articulation of people's worth and ability to know and change the world, forms an essential basis for radical pedagogies in opposition to oppression. Freire's thinking illuminates the central

23. Ibid., 45.

Crossing Borders Intellectually

question of political action in a world that increasingly challenges universals. Freire, like liberation theologians, positions himself on the side of the oppressed; he claims the moral imperative to act in the world. As McLaren has commented in reference to Freire's political stance, "The task of liberating others from their suffering may not emerge from some transcendental fiat, yet it nevertheless compels us to affirm our humanity in solidarity with victims."[24] Freire repeatedly states that this method cannot simply be transferred to other settings, but that each historical site requires the development of pedagogy appropriate to that setting.

Henry Giroux

In order to re-imagine Freire's liberative pedagogy in a more meaningful way, I suggest a focus on a more situated theory of oppression and subjectivity that considers the contradictions in universal claims of truth that his method implies. Among the diversity of available discourses, Henry Giroux's border-crossing pedagogy offers the best means of examining these issues, particularly work that engages a cultural politics of difference.[25] Giroux, who takes postmodern reason as his point of departure, revises Freire's educational projects for the development of contemporary critical pedagogy. Giroux broadly considers reinventing the radicality of Freire's work within an emerging postcolonial discourse.[26] Giroux proposes a synthesis between Freire's

24. McLaren, "Postmodernity and the Death of Politics," 399.

25. Giroux, *Border Crossings*.

26. The term "postcolonialism" is part of a theoretical discourse that is directly related to the once-colonial experience of the colonized. This postcolonial discourse has been contested in the sense that it has various implications, depending on its use and the different areas of application. In dealing with this postcolonial discourse,

An/Other Praxis

unfinished work and that of other postcolonial critics to propose new possibilities.

People of former colonies and present ones are in the process of recovering their stories and rewriting their histories. These new histories expose the colonial agenda within the history of colonial discourse. Giroux understands colonial discourse as one that created the colonized as "Other." It was fundamentally based on essentialism and assumptions associated with Western concepts of modernity[27] such that everything could be categorized into dualistic sets of values: good and evil, central and peripheral, sameness and difference, inside and outside, pure and impure, man and woman, and so on. Based on these exclusive categories, colonial discourse began to define the colonial subject in terms of a "culturally inferior being" or "Other." For example, Western intellectuals have created the term "orient" itself as a cultural construct of thought, images, and practices used by the West to envision and create the oriental Other as integral to the creation of European self-identity and as justification for colonial intervention. Theorist Edward Said called it "orientalism." In his book, *Orientalism*, he exposes the epistemological process of Western thought surround-

---

Giroux considers seriously such works as hooks, *Talking Back*; hooks, *Yearning*; Said, *Orientalism*; Said, *Culture and Imperialism*; and Spivak and Harasym, *Post-Colonial Critic*.

27. The term "modernity" here is not seen simply as a period in time, but as a discourse, "'a highly complex yet coherent narrative containing assumptions' . . . [including] beliefs, characteristics, cultural trends, and rules that define the meaning of modernity . . . This discourse of modernity, then, locates Europe, which becomes the West, at the center of the modern/colonial system and the rest at the periphery" (Martínez-Vázquez, "Breaking the Established Scaffold," 76–77). See also Munslow, *Routledge Companion to Historical Studies*, 163. For a better understanding of this modern colonial system, see Dussel, "Beyond Eurocentrism"; Mignolo, *Darker Side of the Renaissance*; Hall, "West and the Rest."

Crossing Borders Intellectually

ing the colonized, which he believes was based on a political desire for power and found fuller expression in the integration of scientific and information technologies. He defines orientalism simply "as a Western style for dominating, restructuring, and having authority over the orient."[28]

Now, this dominant colonial discourse and the normative history it creates—a history that determines the way people see and interpret the past—is being challenged by postcolonial discourses. Presuming the end of colonialism and inspired by postcolonial theories, Giroux recognizes that the assertion of Western imperialism and its cultural representations form the frame of reference for the term "postcolonial" (as well as "anti-colonial"). With respect to Freire as a border intellectual, Giroux recognizes in this assertion the profound and radical nature of the pedagogical theory and practice of a postcolonial discourse. The term "postcolonialism" represents not a chronological, but instead a critical idea by indicating an intention to go beyond the colonial in all its forms.[29] Postcolonial analysis, under this pedagogy, does highlight the historical effects of the Western empires, in both their settler and exploitation colonies. But it pursues this historical archeology in order to shed light on the aftermath of that imperialism. This aftermath persists.

The postcolonial discourses break epistemological patterns of understanding and knowledge by shifting the role of colonized people from objects of a dominant history to subjects in their own history. While colonial discourses relegate people outside the center of power to the

---

28. Said, *Orientalism*, 2.

29. Giroux, "Politics of Postcolonialism," 177–88. Postcolonial discourse that uses this strategy is similarly found in the works of scholars who study Christianity. For instance, see Segovia, *Interpreting Beyond Borders*.

An/Other Praxis

margins or borders of normative knowledge, postcolonial discourses challenge the normative knowledge to discover subaltern voices. Giroux posits this discovery as a process of uncovering and re-creating one's own cultural memory of the past. It serves the subaltern's quest to form an identity independently from that which had been imposed by colonial heritage. This process of discovery, Giroux argues, can develop a new history informed by uncovered voices and stories long-silenced by the dominant historiographical discourse.

Taking this postcolonial theory as its guiding principle, border-crossing pedagogy serves as a discourse of resistance to any subsequent related projects of dominance. Refusing to reduce the theoretical formulation to the practice of knowledge and skills transmission, Giroux posits "a form of political and cultural production deeply implicated in the construction of knowledge, subjectivities, and social relations."[30] As another kind of post-colonial discourse, border-crossing pedagogy helps to problematize the politics of location situated in the privilege and power of the West. Far from rejecting Freire's goals for what he calls "a cultural practice for liberation," this knowledge production[31] decolonizes the borders that define their own politics of location. In this process of decolonization, theoretical discourse functions as a particular kind of praxis and a particular posture for critiquing dominant social forces. It

---

30. Giroux, *Border Crossings*, 2.

31. The production theory is a mode of discourse that focuses its analysis on issues surrounding how dominant theory and practice are constructed, sustained, and circulated outside of the existing structures. Giroux, for example, says that this production theory is "an important starting point for pedagogy of cultural politics because it evaluates the relationship between institutions and wider structural forces in light of a politics of human dignity" (Giroux, *Pedagogy and the Politics of Hope*, 135–37).

Crossing Borders Intellectually

not only questions received institutions and assumptions, but also opens creative space for subaltern communities to maintain hope against despair and cynicism. In creating this valuable space, the subaltern can articulate more critical discourses. Most importantly, Giroux's border-crossing pedagogy shares Freire's emphasis on seeing human beings as the subjects and not the objects of history.

Rather than getting stuck in a reproductive framework, this transformative way of thinking perceives educational settings as spaces for deconstruction and the development of projects of transformation. This project of transformation is a counter-cultural discourse of critique that moves on to the discourse of possibility that provides the elements to work for change.[32] I observe that many critical educational theories have made available a whole set of empowering categories of inquiry, reconceptualizing this cultural practice for liberation in ways that move away from liberal positions and also transcend reproductive paradigms of critique. But this kind of knowledge production is not a unified and coherent set of ideas. It is more accurate to say that critical theorists, as inspired by Freire, are unified in their objectives: "to empower the powerless and transform existing social inequality and injustice."[33]

Given this objective, Giroux offers four key categories that operate to structure this transformative paradigm.[34] The first is an expansion of the notion of the political as

32. The discourses of critique and possibility are the mode of language that focuses on combination in its critique of domination and its search for new forms of identity and social relations. It also deals with issues of limits with the discourse of freedom and social responsibility. See Giroux, *Teachers as Intellectuals*, 204–22.

33. McLaren, *Life in Schools*, 160.

34. For discussion on the main categories and conceptualizations of critical pedagogy, see Giroux, *Teachers as Intellectuals*; Giroux, *Disturbing Pleasure*; McLaren, "Critical Pedagogy."

permeating the whole social order. Power is understood not only in negative terms, but also in its capacity to create a different social order. The second is the combination of a discourse of critique with one of possibility, empowering subjects to become agents in a process of both social transformation and of reaffirmation in reformulating their histories and experiences in view of more emancipatory concerns. The third is a reconstitution of pedagogical practice, moving it beyond mere technical concerns or elitist professional interests to conceive of the cultural worker as a transformative intellectual who needs to critically engage current social and cultural forms within a wider project of transformation alongside other cultural workers. The final key is contestation of reductionist constructions of any educational institution as neutral space, recognizing it instead as a site of struggle among dominant and subaltern cultural practices along diverse axes of power that can support differences of race, gender, class, and sexual orientation.

These categories create a transformative paradigm that makes it possible to define discursive practices that conceptualize the relationship between culture and pedagogy. What I find empowering about this is that it addresses questions concerning knowledge and identity production as well as their connection within power relations. How knowledge gets produced and communicated and how people participate as subjects in that process constitute fundamental political issues that must be taken into account. All these elements speak to a cultural practice of liberation that is about much more than teaching strategies or practitioners' concerns. Hence, Roger Simon[35] describes this paradigm as a necessary dynamic of theory and practice, with political and ethical concerns leading the process of reflection. This concern should be structured around a fun-

35. Simon, *Teaching Against the Grain*, 3–34.

damental emancipatory discourse of equality, freedom, and justice aimed at a socio-political vision.

Since religious educational traditions in Third World countries are mostly Western, according to the dominant paradigm, questions of pedagogy ignore radical discourses such as Freirean pedagogy and refer exclusively to Eurocentric philosophies of education. Meanwhile, the term "pedagogy" is not commonly understood as a word that relates to critical social theory. It refers instead to a language of technique that articulates discussions about learning, teaching, and educational objectives. What is missing from these dominant cultural approaches is an understanding that pedagogical practices are about much more than abstract philosophical foundations or the technical immediacy of teaching strategies.

Contrary to this dominant position, pedagogical practices as political and cultural praxis are about the kind of socio-political visions they support.[36] Those involved in liberating praxis cannot avoid the fact that these take place in concrete settings within a wider society in which questions of power are articulated. Among such issues: What is to be included and what excluded as legitimate knowledge for learning? Whose story is worth most? What kinds of social relations are being promoted? What forms of learning are articulated, and how do they configure ways of engaging and perceiving ourselves as subjects or passive objects within the world in which we live? What kinds of representations are being constructed of ourselves, of others, and of our physical and social environment?

This mode of inquiry situates us within a completely different tradition as we reinterpret pedagogy as a form of cultural politics. This discursive organization, by acknowledging power as productive, allows us to see how it works

36. Ibid.

An/Other Praxis

through people, knowledge, and desire in a normative way to organize life and its possibilities in a certain form and direction. The tight link between power and culture determines certain modes of semiotic production that are "historically and economically constituted by the social forms within which we live our lives."[37]

Situated by this conceptualization, the term transformative intellectuals should be expanded beyond the limits of the school setting, and best of all, the term "cultural worker"[38] might be an alternative frame for this more liberating perception. After all, pedagogical practices take place within a diversity of modes of cultural production and are engaged in the construction and negotiation of knowledge and identities. Therefore, pedagogical practices speak to broader cultural and social concerns. Pedagogy is about cultural politics. If that is so, pedagogical practices require the involvement of cultural workers to engage in the task of reforming all spheres of cultural production according to a politico-social vision "as part of a wider revitalization of public life."[39]

Given such a context, Giroux argues that critical pedagogy should no longer be understood as "a discipline." Instead, critical pedagogy should be about "the creation of a public sphere, one [praxis] that brings people together in variety of sites to talk, exchange information, listen, feel their desires, and expand their capacities for joy, love, solidarity, and struggle."[40] Giroux's definition underscores

37. Simon, *Teaching Against the Grain*, 76–78.

38. The term "cultural worker" refers to intellectuals who engage in the process of creating symbolic representations that in turn function in the practice of cultural analysis and comprehension. See Giroux, *Border Crossings*, 5, 242–33.

39. Giroux, *Border Crossings*, 242.

40. Giroux, *Disturbing Pleasure*, x.

Crossing Borders Intellectually

the idea that this praxis should be simultaneously about knowledge and practices in the sense that to propose a transformative paradigm is at the same time to construct a socio-political vision.[41] This also implies the importance of theory that takes into account theoretical developments in a diversity of fields within social theory.

The failure to do so produces impoverished reflections and shortsighted political projects with no empowering effect in face of current worldwide challenges. Diverse forms of domination and oppression are calling for a new project of life, and a vision of a better social world. This new vision should be a radical one that speaks to different forms of dissent rather than enforced change, and validates multiple forms of power and authority. A critical pedagogy that produces a true diversity of knowledge and subjectivities by contesting domination and oppression will be a fundamental practice for more egalitarian forms of life.

To establish this transformative social vision, Giroux's border crossing pedagogy offers an empowering articulation of those questions of power that concern postcolonialism, postmodernism, and other liberating theoretical fields that are undergoing radical renewal.[42] In emphasizing these notions, the following chapters argue that analyzing a concrete articulation of theory and experience not only speaks more strongly, but also provides living voices and experiences to explicate this process of reflection. This argument is crucial for a radical imagery that incorporates Giroux's contributions into a proposal for subaltern ways of thinking

41. Ibid., 240.

42. Some of the best resources to understand this transformative pedagogy include Giroux, *Border Crossings*; Giroux, *Postmodernism, Feminism, and Cultural Politics*; Giroux and McLaren, *Between Borders*. See also Spivak, *In Other Worlds*; Lugones and Spelman, "Have We Got a Theory for You!" 573–81; Lugones, "Playfulness," 3–19.

An/Other Praxis

theologically. Those important contributions include the consideration of theoretical ideas of border-crossing praxis in relation to the conception of the subject, practice, experience, and dialogue.

The assumption underlying this analysis is the need to develop a theory by theorizing the practice. Giroux refers to this as theory emerging in concrete settings in order to analyze them critically and put them into action "on the basis of an informed praxis."[43] Such theorizing calls for a language of critique and, at the same time, a language of possibility, not only to recognize injustice, but also to develop a project of emancipation. The need of concepts such as voice, dialogue, and subjectivity in the tradition of critical pedagogy are important not only to deconstruct and reconstruct the terrain of everyday life, but also to develop political action and a sense of agency.

BORDER CROSSINGS AS PERFORMATIVE ACTS

This kind of performative act renames difference through the process of crossing over into cultural borders that address critical questions of experience and agency by emphasizing resistance and by considering the capacity of individuals and groups to demystify dominant cultures. It also offers the possibility of creating new concepts, and of developing a theory to name the subaltern, in this case his or her own subordinated experiences, to make sense of their own lives. The act of border-crossing is, principally, a twofold process: theorizing lived experience and going back to practice with a transformative proposal. This requires that subaltern from different races and cultures engage together

43. Giroux, *Teachers as Intellectuals*, 119.

Crossing Borders Intellectually

in border-crossing theorizing to deal with the concepts of difference, voice, identity, experience, and dialogue. These considerations are the fundamental concepts at work in postcolonial theory. Gayatri Spivak writes that:

> The problem of human discourse is generally seen as articulating itself in the play of three shifting "concepts": language, world, and consciousness. We know no world that is not organized as a language, we operate with no other consciousness but one structured as language—languages that we cannot possess, for those languages operate us as well. The category of language, then, embraces the categories of world and consciousness even as it is determined by them.[44]

This statement points out the role of the discursive in shaping life, but it also stresses the effect of language in focusing theoretical discussion around the need to clarify discourse as part of wider strategy to change the world. Work on discourse and language constitutes an important trend in contemporary social theory. Giroux takes up the issue of language to assert the need for resistance and the possibility of creating new concepts in developing a theory to name the Other, in this case the subaltern experience.

In this process of counter-cultural discourse, the subaltern engage in naming, theorizing, and interpreting personal experiences and demystifying dominant cultures. This not only gives voice to those who have been historically excluded and silenced, but most importantly, re/constructs new pedagogical borders wherein difference becomes the intersection of new forms of culture and identity. Hence, border-crossing praxis suggests more than simply opening diverse cultural histories and spaces to the subaltern. It also

44. Spivak, *In Other Worlds*, 77–78.

means understanding "how fragile identity is as it moves into borderlands crisscrossed with a variety of languages, experiences, and voices."[45]

Regarding this last point, Giroux recognizes border-crossing acts as the only means of theorizing that allows subaltern, who live amid plurality, to express a central need of their ontology and epistemology. In this way the "border intellectuals" focus on the aspects of the subalterns' lives that can address the development of a transformative critical pedagogy of difference. As they cross borders intellectually, they participate in the theory-making process and its articulation in language through dialogue across differences.

It is important to note that individuals are dependent on each other in order to be understood and integrated, and to make sense out of their situation. Being dependent does not mean being subordinated. Rather, being interdependent means being able to cross over the Other's border conceptually in order to offer loving support. Giroux explains that border-crossing intellectually is the concept of moving into circles of uncertainty, crossing into different cultural spheres, and recognizing the multifaceted nature of our own identities. This means understanding and challenging rather than assuming a kind of security within the confines of academic disciplines. Using this concept, we can delineate a borderland as a "construction of life," whether dominant or non-dominant, and can comprehend the relationships of gender and race and other categories of identity that exist in a specific context. This is a powerful approach in that it enables us to consider how life may be represented in a multiplicity of ways.

From a pedagogical perspective, this concept of borderland as lived in the first person is important because it

45. Ibid.

Crossing Borders Intellectually

makes visible the multiplicity of voices, representations, and experiences that make people border-crossers. Crossing, as a relational shift from one side of the borderland to another, not only helps us to get to know and understand one another, it also recognizes the partialities of all discourses, experiences, and codes. It stresses the necessity of becoming border-crossers in order to decenter ourselves and remap meanings, concrete relations, and lives in more egalitarian ways.

This alternate thinking is based on the assumption that power establishes itself in a variety of local sites within and across different pedagogical terrains. Since there is a tendency for one power to dominate others, the act of crossing borders intellectually requires an act of self-reflection. Such self-reflection may lead to the development of strong antagonisms. For instance, developing critical voices that are able to challenge social institutions, legitimize forms of knowledge, and recognize that only certain cultural portraits have been accepted are all activities that may lead to opposition from those in power.

In the Freirean mode of moving education away from the banking notion of passive transmission of knowledge and skills, border-crossers engage in a pedagogical investigation of how these subjectivities have been both produced and manipulated across and within different economic, cultural, and social spheres. By examining the borders that confine them, they become what JanMohamed calls "archaeologists of the site of their own social formation."[46] He says, "As oppressed peoples begin the process of developing strong antagonism and crossing borders, their new subject positions begin to cathect around the project of reading their own social worlds. Thus, their new subjectivities, that is, the construction of knowledge, identities, and social re-

46. JanMohamed, "Paulo Freire's Border Pedagogy," 113–114.

An/Other Praxis

lations, emerges in the process of drawing borders around their old subject positions, a process that constitutes them as progressive border intellectuals."[47]

Theory-Making Process

The purpose of theory is to make sense of life through the use of familiar concepts. Furthermore, a theory is useful if it helps us understand our location in the world using new concepts that do not mystify, but rather, empower us to realize our responsibility for being in that location.

In border-crossing praxis, pedagogical practices are designed to help develop the individual and enable them to see themselves as part of the social order. It reveals how each person functions inside and outside of educational settings, and it works to improve the development of compound identities. The notion of the subject as part of a compound identity indicates a recognition of not only the multiplicity of subject positions—the various roles that each person plays—but also the tensions surrounding them. This praxis of difference not only asserts a multiplicity of voices, but also deconstructs them to reveal how they have become what they are, challenge their problematic assumptions, and reconstruct them.

But pedagogical practices not only construct subjectivities, they also produce knowledge and theory. The question is how to articulate different partialities, different discourses, and different voices in the process of theory-making. Giroux suggests a non-colonial theorizing process that rejects universal claims and reductionism.[48] This theorizing process takes place in other spaces besides the

---

47. Ibid.
48. Giroux, *Border Crossings*, 11–30.

Crossing Borders Intellectually

academy, recognizes partialities, and confronts their limits without excluding those being theorized. In this way, the praxis of difference generates community knowledge to serve all those involved in it, as opposed to a production of knowledge by an elite to serve its own interests.

In his pedagogical theory, Giroux questions the notion of a unified subject moving into history with single identities. He proposes and develops a contrary conception of the constant creation and negotiation of selves within forced structures of ideology. This line of theoretical analysis calls into question assumptions of the common interests of the oppressed. It challenges the use of such universal terms as "oppression" and "liberation" by locating these identity claims in a concrete historical or social context and building coalitions based on recognition of people's partial knowledge of their own constructed identities.[49]

This theoretical formulation of what Giroux calls "multi-layered subjects," along with the need to position identities in relation to their own histories, raises important issues for liberating pedagogies. All identities must be recognized in their full historical and social complexity as in-process subjects, based on knowledges that are always partial and that reflect deep and conflicting differences. If this recognition is acceptable, we can theorize a liberating praxis that actively struggles against different forms of oppression. In doing so, we can build upon a rich and complex analysis that works towards a Freirean vision of social justice and liberation.

---

49. This notion of identity has fueled important work in educational theory. It has helped shape the call for a "border crossing pedagogy" as a critical practice that would enable people to examine their own conditions of existence by adopting "a position of nonidentity with their own positions" (Giroux, *Border Crossings*, 92).

An/Other Praxis

The strength of this theoretical analysis lies in its capacity to foster the principle of social justice based on the importance of the Other and to move the world in the direction of hope, so that it might arch toward the future in a continuing orbit of possibility. As theory, border-crossing praxis offers historical challenges to any forms of ethical decision. Central to this ethical discourse is the need to develop a moral rationality that moves beyond conservative reliance on both essentialist and poststructuralist thought.[50] These intellectual positions subordinate theory to practice, conflate authority with authoritarianism, and reduce language to a vehicle of clarity.

Rejecting such positions, border-crossing praxis posits the importance of theory as a performative act, a politically engaged praxis.[51] It raises a central challenge to the role of cultural workers, deepening their politics through a broader understanding of how knowledge is produced, how identities are formed, and how values are articulated as a pedagogical practice within multiple cultures.

To establish this border-crossing praxis, Giroux proposes the development of an ethical discourse that includes two tasks. First, it must protest against the existing ideological and social praxis, which furthers the mechanisms of power and domination at the level of everyday life. Such protest means moving beyond moral outrage and providing a critical account of how individuals are constituted as human agents within different moral and ethical discourses and experiences. Second, border-crossing praxis must develop a vision of the future that is rooted in the construction of sensibilities and social relations that give meaning to a notion of community that understands democracy as a

50. Giroux, *Border Crossings*, 39–42.

51. For the most important challenges against this intellectualism, see Simon, *Teaching Against the Grain*; Giroux, *Border Crossings*.

Crossing Borders Intellectually

struggle for extending civil rights and improving the quality of human life. This ethical discourse points to a moral rationality that is fundamentally important for formulating pedagogical practices committed to helping individuals free themselves from their socially marginalized lives so that they may define themselves from their own collective imagination.[52]

Experience and Its Articulation in Language

The experience of the subaltern and their articulations in language are important because they relate to the question of identity. Because the subaltern are deeply influenced by what the dominant discourse says about them, their need to hear other voices from within their historical and cultural experience is central to the development of border-crossing praxis. Their daily lives create paths toward self-definition and agency, and these experiences need to be articulated.

The task of border intellectuals is thus to find ways to work with subaltern to enable the full expression of various voices as they engage in dialogue with each other. This suggests that those who work for liberation must find ways to encourage those of different races, classes, and gender positions to speak in self-affirming ways about their experiences. Each person must be able to express how their life has been mediated by their own social position and those of others.

Border-crossing praxis engages experience in order to inquire into the conditions of its production and effects. It raises the question of how experience functions to produce knowledge, and how it might be implicated in the

52. McLaren, *New Information Age*, 32–33. This kind of rationality can be a serious challenge against the community-based theologies that often fail to develop an ethical discourse.

An/Other Praxis

construction of forms of subjectification. Giroux believes that politicizing the relationship between thought and experience points to a pedagogical practice in which cultural workers can offer questions, analyses, visions, and practical options that the subaltern can pursue in their attempts to participate in the determination of various aspects of their lives.

Required here is a practice rooted in an ethico-political vision that attempts to take people beyond the world they already know in a way that does not insist on a fixed set of altered meanings.[53] In this way, border-crossing praxis becomes an attempt to alter experience in the interest of expanding possibilities for human agency and social justice. Thus it makes visible the need for informed social relations that cut across the diverse terrain of cultural studies.

In dealing with this notion, Giroux introduces a particular conception that refers to a multiciplicity of voices.[54] These multilayered voices depend fully upon the positioned subject. But the language consists of social phenomena, always in the process of becoming. Individuals do not receive a ready-made language at all; they enter into social communication and their consciousness is constructed in the process, actively transforming communication. This understanding stresses the role of the individual as well as community in the transformation process.

In exploring the relationship between theory and political action, border intellectuals raise questions about categories and claims for truth that underlie both consciousness-raising and border-crossing pedagogy. Basic to the Freirean method of conscientization is the belief in the

---

53. Giroux, *Politics of Hope*, 169–70. See also Simon, *Teaching Against the Grain*, 46–47.

54. See Giroux, *Postmodernism, Feminism, and Cultural Politics*, 29–30.

Crossing Borders Intellectually

ability of all people to be knowers and to read both the word and the world. This belief is that only through the interrogation of their own experiences will the oppressed come to an understanding of their own power as knowers and so contribute to the transformation of their world. A similar reliance on experience is fundamental to the development of a border-crossing knowledge as the basis for social change. This assumption of experience as the foundation of political analysis and action, as Freirean pedagogy underlines, remains central to border-crossing pedagogy.

Experience is ideologically constructed in the sense that we can only understand it and speak about it in terms of an existing ideology and language. But it is here that Giroux goes beyond Freire in stating that the source of knowledge is not a common or unitary experience, but is found instead in the self-examination of lived experience. Thus, this self-examination can be the basis for an opposition to dominant schemes of truth if experience runs counter to what is set forth and accepted as normatively true.

Hence, the concept of voice offers a pedagogical strategy for negotiating the directiveness of the dominant educational relationship and the political commitment to make the subaltern autonomous in those relationships. This discourse of voice sees the subaltern as empowered when they express their multiple subjugated knowledges.[55] By speaking in their own voices, the subaltern become authors of their world. Such self-definition gives them an identity and political position from which to act as agents of social change.[56]

As a form of cultural politics, discourse surrounding the subaltern experience is not respectful of abstract, universal claims to the truth. On the contrary, it is a discourse

55. Shor and Freire, "What is the 'Dialogical Method'?" 30.
56. Simon, "Empowerment as a Pedagogy," 80.

An/Other Praxis

that allows the subaltern to draw upon their own experiences and cultural resources, enabling them to play a self-consciously active role as producers of knowledge within the teaching and learning process.[57] In this way, Giroux broadens the notion of the political by making it pedagogical, reminding us of the importance of pedagogy as a cultural practice.

In this context, pedagogy deepens and extends the study of culture and power by not only addressing the ways in which culture is shaped, produced, and transformed, but also how it is actually embraced by human beings within specific settings and circumstances. Pedagogy becomes an act of cultural production, a "writing" process in which power is implicated in the production of knowledge, and values begin with real people articulating and rewriting their lived experiences within history.[58] Here the real people can learn to understand how power works differently as both a productive and dominating force, to be able to read the world from a variety of perspectives, and to be willing to think beyond the common-sense assumptions that govern everyday existence.

Dialogue Across Differences

A transformative critical pedagogy addresses difference in all its possibilities within power relations in an effort to contest concrete oppressive practices and interact with specific situations that legitimize the expression of different voices. Giroux sees difference in relational terms that

---

57. Giroux, *Pedagogy and the Politics of Hope*, ch. 5.
58. Ibid., 168–69.

link it to a broader politics that deepen the possibility for reconstructing public spheres.[59]

Therefore, border-crossing praxis posits the need for the outsider and insider to engage in dialogue wherein they are both outsider and insider with respect to one another. Dialogue is a fundamental imperative of ecclesial praxis in order for participants exhibit "trust, sharing, and commitment to improving the quality of human life."[60] Both outsider and insider must agree on the goals of dialogue: "all voices and their differences become unified both in their efforts to identify and recall moments of human suffering and in their attempts to overcome conditions that perpetuate such suffering."[61]

But to engage in dialogue is not to erase differences. Rather, differences are preserved as a precondition for dialogue. Sharon Welch argues that solidarity is not to be confused with absence of difference, because solidarity requires the recognition, understanding, respect, and love that leads people to voice their views in a different way.[62]

Furthermore, crossing borders intellectually requires what feminists call "a playful attitude," meaning a loving way of being and living. Only by adopting this attitude can dialogue bring people to work together across differences. Dialogue becomes a creative form of collective struggle, one that starts with the acknowledgment of unity as interpersonal.[63] If we link the concept of border-crossing praxis to the imperative to engage in dialogue across differences, then border-crossing intellectuals must possess a theo-

59. Giroux, *Border Crossings*, 174.

60. Giroux, "Pedagogy of Voice," 72.

61. Ibid.

62. See Welch, *Communities of Resistance*, 31; cf. Lugones, "Playfulness," 3–19.

63. Martin and Mohanty, "Feminist Politics," 208–209.

retical grasp of the ways in which difference is constructed through various representations and practices that name and exclude the voices of subordinate groups. Particularly, they must address important questions of how these representations and practices are actively learned, challenged, or transformed, and how an understanding of these differences can be used in order to change the prevailing relations of power that sustain them.

Border-crossing intellectuals must also critically interrogate how dominant groups express and sustain understandings of differences through representations that problematize the humanity of the Other. At the same time, they should understand how the everyday experience of subordination lends itself to forms of oppositional and transformative consciousness. Above all, this understanding is based on the need for the Others to reclaim and remake their histories, voices, and visions as part of a wider struggle to change social relations that deny pluralism as the basis of diversity community.[64]

---

64. See Giroux, *Pedagogy and the Politics of Hope*, 156.

5

The *Dhalang* Roles for Transformative Ritual Leadership

> There is no doubt that liberation theology has expanded beyond its ecclesial limits . . . [The subaltern] continue to be a space for theological creativity. They are the collective subjects of theological production. There is intellectual theological creativity, but also a theological creativity at the level of symbols and myths, and in the field of spirituality and popular religiosity.
>
> —Pablo Richard[1]

SCHOLAR VICTOR TURNER UNDERSTANDS rituals as the primary context in which a people interact with their central cultural symbols and so come to understand and be shaped by important values of their community.[2] For

---

1. Richard, "Liberation Theology Today," 28.
2. Turner, *Drums of Affliction*, 2. See also Turner, *Ritual to Theatre*, 79–80.

An/Other Praxis

Turner, rites not only reveal central social and religious values in their present form, but also contain the possibility of transforming human attitudes and behaviors according to these values. This possibility is realized in the performance of these rites, when symbols are manipulated and people interact with supernatural beings or engage in transformative ritual leadership, as is true among my own people, Javanese Protestants, one of many subaltern communities in Indonesia.

We must begin by discussing the present situation of Javanese Protestants. In my view, current worship practices largely function to separate Javanese Christians from important elements of their own cultural traditions. Protestantism came to us as an "imported" religion wedded to Western dogmatism in ways that bluntly forced Javanese Christians to leave behind all remnants of indigenous beliefs by imposing colonial ideologies of the late nineteenth and twentieth centuries. In this period, Javanese culture and history was contaminated by the imposition of the ideological interpretations of colonial Dutch East Indies authorities.

In his ethnographic study of Java, John Pemberton shows how the European celebration of "progress" and colonial technologies of surveillance both seduced and constricted the movement of members of the Javanese elite into domains defined by Dutch control.[3] Pemberton cites examples of versions of ancient texts describing Javanese rituals and customs such as royal processions, weddings, wedding attire, and marriage alliances that demonstrate the ambivalence of Javanese authors struggling to come to terms with Dutch power and presence.[4] By contrasting this situation with pre-colonial texts, Pemberton asserts that the

3. Pemberton, *Subject of "Java,"* 106.
4. Ibid., 333.

The Dhalang Roles for Transformative Ritual Leadership

quotation marks that make Java into "Java" slowly reveal their meaning as they appear along with the reconstruction of readings of Indonesian culture and history that enable political repression. "Java" exists in tension with colonial and postcolonial efforts to co-op texts and rituals to serve the needs of totalizing state power.[5]

As a result of this historical situation, Javanese Christianity often falls into two kinds of "handcuffs," namely the "Egypt" handcuff and the "Zion" handcuff.[6] The first describes the ways in which Christianity has become impotent in its responses to the social realities now operating in Indonesia. The second exposes the internal contradictions of the churches, problems that are ideological.[7] To be free of these handcuffs, Javanese Christianity requires what Berger calls a new exodus. In the spirit of a new and "transformative" exodus, I will utilize Turner's theory of ritual to interpret (or reposition) the relationship between Javanese Christians and other ritual traditions in Indonesia. Rather than maintaining an oppositional stance toward in-

---

5. Ibid.

6. I borrow this metaphor from Peter L. Berger to identify the problems that need to be transformed. See Berger, *Precarious Vision*, 8–22, 102–26.

7. The use of the term "ideology" is problematic when it does not recognize both the dominant paradigm and its active opposition in cultural struggle, namely the ways in which subordinate groups (e.g., Javanese Christians) confront the hegemonic products of the social or intellectual elite (e.g., Western Protestants). Following Antonio Gramsci's work on the concept of hegemony, I see the Protestant Church as a socio-religious institution that can and should be held responsible for the production, reproduction, and transformation of hegemony. Such a notion opposes ways of understanding a situation in which the investigator pays too much attention to the use of coercion, focusing exclusively on the coercive power of the dominant group in relation to economic factors while excluding factors related to cultural struggles. See Mouffe, "Hegemony and Ideology," 182–83.

digenous beliefs and practices, my claim is that figures such as the *dhalangs* of the Javanese shadow theater can serve as models of ritual leadership for the churches.

A central concept in Turner's ritual theory is liminality. I consider both *dhalangs*, the clowns of the shadow theater, and Javanese Christians to be liminal figures and liminal communities. Like *dhalangs*, Javanese Christians are loyal to their traditions, yet they are nevertheless marginalized within Javanese society in generally and in the Protestant Church particularly. As in Turner's "liminal phase," they are the first generation of Christians in transition from "primitive" to "modern" religion (i.e., Christianity). Turner describes those in this phase as "betwixt and between" with characteristics that are essentially ambiguous.[8] In such a condition, syncretism, which is an essential part of the ritual performance of Javanese Christians, should not be interpreted as the threat that missionary Protestantism considered it to be, but rather as the "creative" action of Javanese Christians attempting to escape from the crisis of the loss of their cultural moorings. As a creative action, experiments in syncretism (like the one I attempt here) serve both as a critique of the anti-Javanese attitude of many church leaders and as an attempt to secure a Javanese Christian identity.

But what about the liminality of the *dhalangs* of shadow theater? The Javanese shadow theater, or the *wayang*, puppet show is a central cultural institution in Indonesia. It is also a popular form of entertainment. But its popularity should not obscure its importance to the philosophical life and beliefs of the Javanese people, including Javanese Christians. For hundreds of years, the Javanese people have recognized the shadow theater as the source of indigenous philosophy and spirituality.

8. Turner, "Betwixt and Between," 4.

The Dhalang *Roles for Transformative Ritual Leadership*

As a cultural art form, the shadow theater is a medium of mass communication, transmitting core values and moral advice with each performance in the form of cultural symbols. Laurie J. Sears recognizes the shadow theater as "the dominant expression of a Javanese philosophy, religion, and worldview."[9] At the same time, the shadow theater has historically been influenced by the ideologies of colonialism. Sears argues that performances of *wayang* shows have been influenced both by the current regime's efforts to control their message and by the mass media's "telling" of them in print.[10]

The leader of the shadow theater is *Ki dhalang*. In every show, someone must assume the role of *dhalang*, the leader of the performance. The title *dhalang* comes from the words for "skilled storyteller." Although those who take the role of *dhalang* are marginalized people in society, during the performance, his or her character becomes a transformative figure for the audience.

I contend that Javanese Christians would do well to attend to the phenomenon of these subordinated *dhalangs*, and especially to the ways in which they function in this ritual context. As they lead a performance of the sacred story, *Punakawan*, the *dhalangs* take the role of loyal servant clowns who come from *kahayangan* ("heaven") and function as ritual specialists and/or as mediators in other social realms. Such a model of leadership from the marginalized is also crucial for transformative leadership in Protestant churches. Church leaders should learn from the *dhalang* who are able to embody the clown, *Semar*, a powerful and transformative figure.

---

9. Sears, *Shadows of Empire*, 11.
10. Ibid., 12.

An/Other Praxis

THE RELATIONSHIP BETWEEN RITUAL AND RELIGIOUS BELIEF IN TURNER

Turner lived and worked for many years among the Ndembu people, examining the cultural field and analyzing Ndembu religious belief. He came to distinguish two components of religion: belief (religion as thought) and practice (religion as ritual action) and offered numerous detailed analyses of ritual performances. In discussing Ndembu religious belief, we see that religion for Turner, as in the work of Claude Lévi-Strauss, was primarily "religion in action."[11] In other words, religion is what religion does. Its power is manifest (or not) depending on how generative it is for sustaining human life. In this sense, religion is known primarily through its rites.

Accepting Turner's distinction between belief and practice, it seems to me that whenever ritual is inspired by religious belief in supernatural beings or powers, its status becomes different from other, inner-worldly forms of knowledge. For people who participate in a variety of ritual activities, religious beliefs have some kind of "surplus value" over and above other secular forms of thought. In this way, religion is not like any other system of ideas and so carries supreme ontological value, but as Turner notes, only for those who "do" the rites of that religion.

Ritual is generally understood in terms of the narrative it contains or communicates. Under this model, the narrative receives the primary emphasis, and ritual is simply a way of expressing the story. This emphasis on the narrative structure of ritual is related to views of the self that emphasize the self as narratively constructed.[12]

---

11. Turner, *Drums of Affliction*, 14–15.
12. See Turner, *Ritual to Theatre*, 79.

The Dhalang *Roles for Transformative Ritual Leadership*

Extending this perspective, Turner suggests that ritual is a social process. In Turner's view, rituals help people to move from disruption to resolution, from disorder back to order. But such a return to order does not always mean a return to the way things were. Turner also suggests that the temporal structure of rituals of resistance shed light on rituals' capacity to resist the official social order.

The narrative approach to self and ritual has been criticized in recent scholarly debate surrounding space and transformation. For instance, in his discussion of issues of ritual transformation Robert Moore argues that Turner did not pay sufficient attention to the dynamics of modern social and religious institutions.[13] Using a contemporary psychotherapeutic approach, Moore proposes a new agenda: "a wide-ranging rethinking of the nature of the relationship between *homo religious*, sacred space, and ritual leadership."[14] Moore adds that this new agenda should focus on modern rituals of initiation that still contain many elements of domination and oppression.

However, I argue that many marginalized people and groups do not experience "reality" as a process that moves from disruption to restoration and consequently view ritual differently than Turner does. An analysis of Javanese Christianity and the shadow theater will challenge Turner's assumptions. Furthermore, I question Turner's ability to apply insights from his studies of the Ndembu to other societies, both contemporary and historical.[15] His interest in liminality and liminal symbols in the context of the processual structure of rituals led Turner to consider this phenomenon in relation to marginal social groups. Because he

13. Moore, "Space and Transformation," 141.

14. Ibid., 141.

15. See Turner, *Ritual Process*, 44–93. See also Turner, *Dramas, Fields, and Metaphors*.

understands ritual to be a form of communication, Turner proposes that theories relating to the processual structure of ritual and rituals' relationship to "social dramas" could illuminate our understanding of certain cultural identities.[16]

With these caveats in mind, I recognize that Turner's work has been influential in recent developments in cultural studies. As is evident in the following pages, his ideas have also significantly influenced my own interpretations. Since my aim in this work is to shed light on how we may understand the nature of the subaltern group represented by the case of Christian Javanese tradition, I begin with a working definition of marginality, borrowed from Turner. This definition distinguishes between "outsidership" and "marginality" as follows:

> the state of outsidership [refers] to the condition of being either permanently and by ascription set outside the structural arrangements of a given social system, or being situationally or temporarily set apart, or voluntarily setting oneself apart from the behavior of status-occupying, role-playing members of that system . . . [Such "outsiders"] should be distinguished from "marginals," who are simultaneously members (by ascription, optation, self-definition, or achievement) of two or more groups whose social definitions and cultural norms are distinct from, and often even opposed to, one another . . . What is interesting about such marginals is that they often look to their group of origin, the so-called inferior group, for *communitas*, and to the more prestigious group in which they mainly live and in which they aspire to higher status as their structural reference group. Sometimes

---

16. Turner, *Ritual Process*, 94–130.

The Dhalang *Roles for Transformative Ritual Leadership*

they become radical critics of structure from the perspective of *communitas*.[17]

JAVANESE CHRISTIANITY AND A RECONSTRUCTION OF SYNCRETISM

Syncretism is a technical term with substantial negative connotations in religious or theological contexts. It is commonly used to refer to combining or merging different religions or beliefs. Such merging is understood to reduce the distinctiveness of each religion. Based on this negative connotation, Protestant institutions see syncretism as a problem to be avoided. Even today, church authorities accuse Javanese Christians of not being fully Christian. To eliminate syncretism, many churches offer ways to purify Javanese Christianity from syncretism. Often, these new ways seem to be more about compulsion than clarification.

I contend that the narrow understanding of syncretism predominant in Protestant doctrine is no longer helpful in contemporary Christianity. Based on Turner's concept of ritual process, we can no longer understand cultural or religious experiences as depending on one particular spiritual source alone. Rather, we need to broaden our view to see that these religious experiences originate from a spiritual mentality that contains complex symbols. In discussing the properties of ritual symbols, Turner asserts that:

> A single symbol, in fact, represents many things at the same time: it is multivocal, not univocal. Its references are not all of the same logical order but are drawn from many domains of social experience and ethical [spiritual] evaluation . . . symbols, then, unite the organic with the

17. Turner, *Drama, Fields, and Metaphors*, 233.

sociomoral order, proclaiming their ultimate religious unity, over and above conflicts between and within these orders.[18]

I am convinced that such experiences of symbolic multivocality elude those who emphasize orthodoxy alone. When Protestant churches of Indonesia encounter Javanese culture, a monotheistic, imported Christianity comes in conflict with Javanese beliefs that focus strongly on *flexibility*. Javanese culture's syncretization of the imported religion has, however, reduced the rigidity of its orthodox religious doctrines. Thus, Javanese Christianity is in a complicated situation, living with the tension of orthodox doctrines while following traditional ways of life that have been syncretistically rooted in the personality of the Javanese people for centuries.

One might well ask which has played the more significant role in the process of acculturation: the Javanese way of life or Christianity? Will Christianity be absorbed in the Javanese culture or vice versa? Should the Javanese people leave behind their own culture, which has served as their firm foundation for centuries?

In my opinion, syncretism, in the context of Javanese culture, is a natural tendency. Javanese Christians naturally accept new elements while consistently adhering to traditional ones. In the Protestant Church, such an attitude can be understood as what Turner terms "anti-structure." Turner explains,

> I have used the term "anti-structure" . . . to describe both liminality and what I have called "communitas." I meant by it not a structural reversal . . . but the liberation of human capacities of cognition, affect, volition, creativity, etc., from

18. Turner, *Ritual Process*, 52–53.

The Dhalang *Roles for Transformative Ritual Leadership*

the normative constraints incumbent upon occupying a sequence of social statuses.[19]

Thus, Javanese Christians can be categorized as people who are in a liminal phase. I argue that because syncretism is a typical characteristic of the Javanese people, such liminality should be classified as a *permanent* symbol.[20] It is permanent because the syncretistic attitude is inherent in the identity of the Javanese people.

We might then construe, as I have noted, syncretism as a creative attitude of Javanese Christians. Javanese Protestants should no longer depend fully on the Western Protestant tradition. However, this creative attitude is also a *critique* of Protestant leaders who refuse to descend into this liminal experience of the church. Javanese syncreticism does not only merge and mix different religious or cultural elements, both old and new, it also attempts to combine and reconcile imbalances. This attempt to integrate different religious or cultural elements in turn produces a new element.[21] Thus, it is possible that syncretism may produce a kind of new religion (for instance, a new form of Christianity or Islam) that contains or mixes various older beliefs, or it could produce a "new" belief that will not be recognizable as Christianity, Islam, Buddhism, or Hinduism.

The Javanese people are best described by the proverb: "*wong Java iku nggoning semu*," a saying that means the Javanese people are the source of all symbols. That is, the Javanese are said to be able to understand all human characters directly through symbols, without any explanation. In other words, the Javanese people have enough sense of *tepa*

19. Turner, *Ritual to Theatre*, 44.

20. In my view, Turner did not find any model of liminality in his Ndembu ritual studies. Nevertheless, in many things, he recognizes the cultural uniqueness in his ritual studies.

21. Kraemer, *Christian Faith*, 392.

An/Other Praxis

salira ("feeling") to show respectful restraint toward one another with the symbolic sympathy of Javanese cultural openness. This also means that they tend to be attentive to and appreciative of others—not just towards their own people or culture, but members of other cultures as well. For this reason, the Javanese people are, in general, friendly with everyone they encounter, for friendliness is one of the prominent characteristics of the Javanese people in daily life. This cultural trait is often manifested in the sacrifice of self-interest for the sake of others out of respect for their cultural symbols. This is also the reason why the Javanese people tend to view any religion or belief positively.[22]

With this understanding these basic attitudes of the Javanese people, we can better understand Javanese Christians, who share the same tendencies of Javanese people in general. They cannot fully let go of their old ritual traditions and exhibit a high tolerance for new beliefs.

Appreciating the religious and cultural elements of others has its benefits. The Javanese themselves are convinced that such tolerance psychologically protects them from many shocks. They almost never place structured practices in opposition to new things. These are long-standing habits dating from historical encounters with foreign cultures and religions such as Islam, Christianity, Buddhism, and Hinduism. This is not to say that every past cross-cultural encounter went smoothly. For instance, the Javanese took two quite different approaches in encountering Christianity. Some who accepted Christianity wanted to be known as "the Javanese Christians," while others named themselves "the Dutch Christians."

Thus, I can conclude that the proper response to the problem of syncretism in Javanese Christianity is not either a "yes" or "no" answer, but instead a question of "how," for

22. See Geertz, *Interpretation of Cultures*.

The Dhalang *Roles for Transformative Ritual Leadership*

syncretism is an essential part of life for Javanese Christianity. Syncretism, the reconciliation between old and new religious elements, is *typical* for Javanese Christianity and should not be avoided. Merging Christian convictions and Javanese traditions of ritual performance and leadership will strengthen, rather than threaten, the health of Javanese Protestantism.

JAVANESE SHADOW THEATER

The shadow theater is an ancient art native to the people of the island of Java, and in my opinion, serves as a symbol of transformation of human life in solidarity with the oppressed, bestowing a spirit of freedom upon them. The shows are very popular because each performance contains sacred values. The Javanese people are convinced that these *wayang* shows also function as a processual ritual. For example, the symbol *gunungan* ("mountain") is an important component of every *wayang* performance. Symbolizing the power of the creator, *gunungan* is used to begin the play, during the change from one scene to another, or in conjunction with images such as the wind, an obstacle, clouds, or seas.

Before commencing a *wayang* performance, a set of traditional offerings are prepared with incense burning and a prayer to God Almighty to ask that the *wayang* performance be conducted safely and that the message be accepted by the audience. The contents of the story are taken from the epics of *Ramayana* and *Mahabharata*, originally from India. In each show, the *dhalang*, or lead actor, gives moral advice based on each character. In fact, these epics contain many spiritual messages. Nevertheless, in Javanese shadow theater, the stories have changed to emphasize the role of the Javanese ancestors over time. Every *wayang* show follows a basic pattern. First there is a court audience, followed by a battle between *ksatria* ("prince") and *buto* ("giants"), who are led by *Buto Cakil*. The *ksatria* wins the battle by killing *Buto Cakil*, symbolizing that every good effort should end successfully after eliminating obstacles. Next, the famous *Punakawan* appears in a sequence that is marked by comedy, songs, and music. The *dhalang* perform the role of these loyal servant clowns, who come from *kahayangan* ("heaven"). The *Punakawan*'s names are *Semar* (whose gender is unclear) and his/her disciples, *Gareng*, *Petruk*, and *Bagong*.

The *Punakawan* joke most of the time and ridicule each other, but they also reflect wisdom and truth. *Semar* is a *guru* ("teacher") who is assigned to live on the earth in order to serve as an escort to the *ksatria*. The figures of *Semar* and *Punakawan* are unique to Javanese *wayang*. The name *Semar* comes from *sengsem* ("to lure") and *marsudi* ("to search, to do") and means "one who is lured to search for or to do good things." *Semar* has come to be understood as a symbol of knowledge, and not just any knowledge, but *gati* ("true and correct knowledge"). *Semar* is a wise person who always teaches a true and correct lesson.

The four *Punakawan*, to the end, symbolize the four sources of true knowledge: the wise teacher, good leaders, one's own experiences, and divine inspiration. They symbolize ordinary poor people with divine knowledge and behavior. Although the *Punakawan* are only humble servants, they become decision-makers and play a leading role. They can be seen from many different angles—many of which would reduce their potential to serve as models of transformative leadership. Some see them merely as entertaining, but others, namely those with privilege and social power, recognize the potency of the clowns but tame them to appropriate as propagandistic tools for their own purpose.

The Dhalang *Roles for Transformative Ritual Leadership*

The *Punakawan* are not followers of the rulers or leaders. They are correctly viewed as *pamong wong cilik* ("guardians of the grassroots") because they place the common people's complaints, needs, and will before rulers or leaders. Their speeches usually contain critical allusions to actual conditions. Their humor stems from grassroots reactions to, or critiques of, real leaders. In other words, the *Punakawan* symbolize the solidarity of the heavens with the people.

Anthropologically, the *Punakawan* tend to be portrayed as servants, as less than the princes with whom they banter as literary characters. A broad survey of global writings reveals that this familiar model is one among several—in some traditions, clowns dominate others, as with Shakespeare's Falstaff. Nevertheless, in the case of Indonesia, the dynamic of clown below prince reflects a socio-political design in which institutional leaders oppress the people. Obviously, those who benefit at the top of the social hierarchy would prefer to let the people become increasingly marginalized rather than descend to solidarity with them. Moreover, such static notions of harmony are recognized as an important part of society's grand narrative,[23] which supports hierarchical and oppressive social structures. Thus, the existing social harmony is legitimated through literary readings that also narrate a cosmic harmony.

Within this context, I think Turner's contributions to ritual theory are welcome and important, for his concept of liminality is useful in interrupting oppressive hierarchical harmony. From the standpoint of the liminal, the clown narratives speak for the marginalized in ways that successfully reach through to the ears of those at the center. These participative voices can get away with making radical

---

23. The term "grand narrative" is typical terminology in the realm of postmodern theory.

critiques of the dominant order and oppressive leaders in and through the drama. Clifford Geertz is correct when he writes: "But what, finally, of Semar, in whom so many oppositions seem to meet—the figure who is both god and clown, man's guardian spirit and his servant, the most spiritually refined inwardly and the most rough-looking outwardly? . . . Like Falstaff, he is fat, funny, and worldly-wise; and, like Falstaff, he seems to provide in his vigorous amoralism a general criticism of the very values the drama affirms."[24] In this way, the *Punakawan*, in my opinion, serve as an important symbol of transformation of human life that is in solidarity with the oppressed, and bestows upon them a spirit of freedom.

The Dhalang of the Shadow Theater

In the shadow theater, the *dhalang* position is very important. He or she leads the performance as its overall artist. As such, the *dhalang* must have a broad knowledge of several disciplines, such as:

1. Deep mastery of *wayang*, the epics of *Ramayana* as well as *Mahabharata*, and the characters of *wayang* figures;
2. Javanese philosophy, moral ethics, and their interconnections;
3. A broad understanding of many aspects of life in the country;
4. Public speaking, or the capacity to imitate about 80 *wayang* figures with different voices;
5. The ability to prepare the scenario;
6. Mastery of the *gamelan*, Javanese musical

24. Geertz, *Interpretation of Cultures*, 139.

The Dhalang Roles for Transformative Ritual Leadership

instruments used to accompany the show, as the *dhalang* must conduct the *gamelan* music;

7. Choral direction, since the *dhalang* leads the chorus of *pesinden*, male and female singers;

8. Puppetry, for the *dhalang* must move the puppets skillfully;

9. Comic timing, as the *dhalang* has to know how to tell good jokes that subtly advise the audience.[25]

The role of *dhalang* is very important because a *dhalang* is the director and the main player of the show. Besides moving the puppets, the *dhalang* also gives them voice—and so serves simultaneously as a comedian and a preacher of spiritual teachings. The demands on a *dhalang* are not only physical, but spiritual as well. A *dhalang* must be able to *mumpuni* ("set an example for others"), a high standard of spirituality among the Javanese. Before a show begins, a *dhalang* undertakes ascetic practices, among which meditation is central.[26] Patricia Henry asserts that the goal of this meditation is to meet the "god within," to become one with the Absolute of undifferentiated reality (as opposed to the differentiated reality of the phenomenal world). This experience of unification conveys power and *sakti* ("holiness") to the adept. According to Hindu tradition, *tapa* ("meditation") ultimately aims at achieving *moksa* ("release," or *nirvana*) from the cycle of rebirth, but as Henry argues, this release removes one completely from the phenomenal world, so there are intermediate goals.[27] Through such exercises, a *dhalang* is believed to be able to commune between

---

25. Glascock et al., *Wayang Kulit*, (Lebanon, NH: American Gamelan Institute, 1997), VHS.

26. Meditation, or *tapa*, comes from Indic tradition. See Henry, "Religion of Balance," 100.

27. Ibid., 101–102.

An/Other Praxis

the physical and spiritual world during shows and is therefore able to comprehend and communicate the meaning of the various symbols.

In the shadow theater, the *dhalang* effects transformation, serving in the symbolic role of mediator. Because of this, the *dhalang* can serve as a metaphor for the kind of transformative leadership that is needed in Christian communities to create communitas, the space for transformative ministry. Such mediation is also central in Christianity. Just as the marginalized *dhalang* serves the community as a skilled ritual leader, and just as mediatory roles are often assigned to individuals from marginalized social groups (such as Martin Luther King Jr. and Mahatma Gandhi), so too might the Christian community serve important mediating functions among the more dominant groups with whom they are marginally related.[28]

A *dhalang* weaves together various spiritual messages, motivating audiences to act upon spiritual values from more than one religious source. On most occasions, the *dhalang* plays a role as mouthpiece of the sponsors. In a performance organized by the Agency of Family Planning, he or she is expected to raise issues related to family planning. In front of the armed forces, the *dhalang* speaks of leadership and discipline. In front of young people, he or she speaks of knowledge, good conduct, and the goals of life. The topics might be different, but the modes of communication are similar: the *dhalang* uses humor lavishly and conducts moral lessons between songs sung by the *pesinden* and *gamelan* music. The *dhalang*'s moral advice is inserted throughout the show: encouraging hard work, insisting that every deed must be conducted properly, and

28. Turner, *Ritual Process*, 96. See also Turner, *Drama, Fields, and Metaphors*, 231–33.

The Dhalang *Roles for Transformative Ritual Leadership*

reminding the audience not to hurt another's feelings, and not to break laws, especially the highest law, the law of God.

Through these heavily symbolic performances, the *dhalang* can also address significant issues in Javanese social and religious history—including contemporary crises and ongoing oppressive forces. Such crises create, on a large scale, a "liminal" state that must be addressed through a transformative process that often entails purification. Because the *dhalang* is able to dialogue with supernatural powers, such as the clown *Semar*, he or she can provide the audience with direction in making decisions and facilitate purification and transformation. Beyond this, the *dhalang* is also able to persuade and invite the audience to be active in fighting against wickedness, and so transform their lives.

An important feature of the epic stories on which the puppet shows are based is their flexibility, their ability to shift in meaning as the social context changes. New meanings continually adhere to old stories. In this, of course, they do not differ from other symbolic statements, which is what all allegories effectively are. The meaning of symbols is dependent on the understandings that the audience brings to them, making symbols multivocal and giving them great communicative powers. The meaning of the stories, therefore, is not fixed, but instead changes with context and audience. Sears sums up this notion admirably when she writes that the tales are seen as "waves in an ocean of stories that absorbs and carries the stories along through the centuries."[29] This "ocean" contains not just the *wayang* stories themselves, but also the scholarly commentaries that have influenced them in every era, including the present one.

---

29. Sears, *Shadows of Empire*, 190–91.

An/Other Praxis

THE DHALANG ROLES IN ECCLESIAL PRAXIS

We should recognize that the existing ecclesial praxis rarely causes people to experience what Turner calls "liminality." We fail to give those within, or those outside of, our churches the opportunity to express to explore alternatives to the meaninglessness, alienation, and injustice of their lives. If the church's theology and practices are to have such effects, church leaders must side with the subaltern. Max Horkheimer, one of the proponents of the Frankfurt School, writes:

> Theology . . . is the hope that this injustice by which the world is characterized is not permanent, that injustice may not be the last word. It is the expression of a longing that the murderer may not triumph over his innocent victim.[30]

Without fail, church leaders must join in becoming partners with those who are dehumanized. Churches must join the struggle for re-humanization, empowering the subaltern to voice and act on their discontent. The *dhalang* offers to the churches an effective model of contextual spirituality. In the teachings of these clowns, attitudes of prophetic critique and solidarity are primary.

Adopting this theologically creative model will not be easy or come without risk. It will necessitate a transformation in church structures that are used to establish the privileged in living comfortably amidst injustice. Just like Turner says, critique requires moments of "anti-structure" in order to come to consciousness and voice. The clown is inherently anti-ideological and anti-establishment. So if we adopt the role of the *dhalang* as a model for ministry, we can

---

30. Quoted in Moltmann, *Theology Today*, 90.

The Dhalang *Roles for Transformative Ritual Leadership*

be certain that this is not a model that comforts and obeys the structures of policy. Instead, as a model of ministry, of the clown life, it sharply critiques the structural policy of the Christian Church and its seeming partiality towards the powerful.

Bibliography

Agamben, Giorgio. *The Time That Remains: A Commentary on the Letter to the Romans*. Translated by Patricia Dailey. Stanford: Stanford University Press, 2005.

Althaus-Reid, Marcella. "From Liberation Theology to Indecent Theology." In *Latin American Liberation Theology: The Next Generation*, edited by Ivan Petrella, 20–38. Maryknoll, NY: Orbis, 2005.

Althusser, Louis. "Ideology and the Ideological State Apparatuses." In *Lenin and Philosophy, and Other Essays*. Translated by Ben Brewster, 127–87. New York: Monthly Review, 1971.

Anzaldúa, Gloria. *Borderlands/La Frontera: The New Mestiza*. San Francisco: Aunt Lute, 1987.

Apple, Michael. *Ideology and Curriculum*. London: Routledge, 1979.

Badiou, Alain. *Saint Paul: The Foundation of Universalism*. Cultural Memory in the Present. Stanford: Stanford University Press, 1997.

Bakhtin, Mikhail. *The Dialogic Imagination: Four Essays*. Edited by Michael Holquist and translated by Caryl Emerson and Michael Holquist. Slavic Series 1. Austin: University of Texas Press, 1981.

Barth, Karl. *The Epistle to the Romans*. Oxford: Oxford University Press, 1933.

Berger, Peter L. *The Precarious Vision: A Sociologist Looks at Social Fictions and Christian Faith*. Westport, CT: Greenwood, 1976.

Bhabha, Hommi. *Location of Culture*. New York: Routledge, 1994.

Boff, Clodovis. *Theology and Praxis: Epistemological Foundations*. Translated by Robert Barr. Maryknoll, NY: Orbis, 1987.

Boff, Leonardo. *Church: Charism and Power: Liberation Theology and the Institutional Church*. Translated by John W. Diercksmeier. New York: Crossroad, 1986.

———. *Ecclesiogenesis: The Base Communities Reinvent the Church*. Translated by Robert R. Barr. Maryknoll, NY: Orbis, 1986.

Bibliography

Bourdieu, Pierre, and Jean-Claude Passeron. *Reproduction in Education, Society, and Culture.* Theory, Culture, and Society. Thousand Oaks, CA: Sage, 1977.

Bowles, Samuel, and Herbert Gintis. *Schooling in Capitalist America: Educational Reform and the Contradictions of Economic Life.* New York: Basic, 1976.

Brueggemann, Walter. *The Prophetic Imagination.* Philadelphia: Fortress, 1978.

Bultmann, Rudolph. *Jesus and the Word.* New York: Scribner, 1962.

Chopp, Rebecca S. "Introduction: Crisis, Hope, and Contextual Theology." In *Reconstructing Christian Theology*, edited by Rebecca S. Chopp and Mark L. Taylor, 1–24. Minneapolis: Fortress, 1994.

———. "Latin American Liberation Theology." In vol. 2 of *The Modern Theologies: Introduction to Christian Theology in the Twentieth Century*, edited by David Ford, 171–92. Oxford: Blackwell, 1995.

———. *The Praxis of Suffering: An Interpretation of Liberation and Political Theologies.* Maryknoll, NY: Orbis, 1986.

Cone, James. *A Black Theology of Liberation.* Philadelphia: J. B. Lippincott, 1970.

Deleuze, Gilles, and Felix Guattari. *A Thousand Plateaus: Capitalism and Schizophrenia.* Translated by Brian Massumi. Minneapolis: University of Minnesota Press, 1987.

Dussel, Enrique. "Beyond Eurocentrism: The World-System and the Limits of Modernity." In *The Cultures of Globalization*, edited by Fredric Jameson and Masao Miyoshi, 3–31. Durham: Duke University Press, 1998.

Eagleton, Terry. *The Illusion of Postmodernism.* Cambridge, MA: Blackwell, 1996.

Fanon, Frantz. *Black Skin, White Masks.* New York: Grove, 1967.

———. "On National Culture." In *The Wretched of the Earth*, translated by Constance Farrington, 145–169. New York: Grove, 1963.

Feibleman, James Kern. *Education and Civilization: The Transmission of Culture.* Dordrecht, Netherlands: Martinus Nijhoff, 1987.

Freire, Paulo. *Education for Critical Consciousness.* New York: Seabury, 1973.

———. *Education: The Practice of Freedom.* London: Writers and Readers Publishing Cooperative, 1973.

———. *The Politics of Education: Culture, Power, and Liberation.* Translated by Donaldo Macedo. Westport, CT: Bergin & Garvey, 1985.

Bibliography

———. *Pedagogy of the Oppressed*. Translated by Myra Bergman Ramos. 30th anniv. ed. New York: Continuum, 2000.

Freire, Paulo, and Donaldo P. Macedo. *Literacy: Reading the Word and the World*. Critical Studies in Education. South Hadley, MA: Bergin & Garvey, 1987.

Fulkerson, Mary McClintock. *Changing the Subject: Women's Discourse and Feminist Theology*. Minneapolis: Fortress, 1994.

———. "Contesting Feminist Canons: Discourse and the Problem of Sexist Texts." *Journal of Feminist Studies in Religion* 7 (1991) 53–73.

Geertz, Clifford. *The Interpretation of Cultures*. New York: Basic, 1973.

Giroux, Henry A. *Border Crossings: Cultural Workers and the Politics of Education*. New York: Routledge, 1992.

———. "Cultural Studies as Performative Politics." *Cultural Studies <=> Critical Methodologies* 1 (2001) 5–23.

———. *Disturbing Pleasure: Learning Popular Culture*. New York: Routledge, 1994.

———. "Literacy and the Pedagogy of Voice and Political Empowerment." *Educational Theory* 38 (1988) 61–75.

———. *Living Dangerously: Multiculturalism and the Politics of Difference*. Counterpoints 1. New York: P. Lang, 1993.

———. "Paulo Freire and the Politics of Postcolonialism." In *Paulo Freire: A Critical Encounter*, edited by Peter McLaren and Peter Leonard, 177–88. New York: Routledge, 1993.

———. *Pedagogy and the Politics of Hope: Theory, Culture, and Schooling; A Critical Reader*. Edge, Critical Studies in Educational Theory. Boulder, CO: Westview, 1997.

———. "Resisting Difference: Cultural Studies and the Discourse of Critical Pedagogy." In vol. 4 of *Cultural Studies*, edited by Lawrence Grossberg et al., 199–212. New York: Routledge, 1992.

———. *Teachers as Intellectuals: Toward a Critical Pedagogy of Learning*. Critical Studies in Education. Westport, CT: Bergin & Garvey, 1988.

———. "Theories of Reproduction and Resistance in the New Sociology of Education: A Critical Analysis." *Harvard Educational Review* 53 (1983) 257–93.

———. *Theory and Resistance in Education: A Pedagogy for the Opposition*. Critical Perspectives in Social Theory. South Hadley, MA: Bergin & Garvey, 1983.

———, editor. *Postmodernism, Feminism, and Cultural Politics: Redrawing Educational Boundaries*. Teacher Empowerment and

Bibliography

School Reform. Albany: State University of New York Press, 1991.

Giroux, Henry A., and Stanley Aronowitz. *Education Under Siege: The Conservative, Liberal, and Radical Debate over Schooling.* Critical Studies in Education. South Hadley, MA: Bergin & Garvey, 1985.

Giroux, Henry A., and Peter McLaren, editors. *Between Borders: Pedagogy and the Politics of Cultural Studies.* New York: Routledge, 1994.

Glascock, Baylis, et al. *Wayang Kulit: The Shadow Puppet Theatre of Java.* Lebanon, NH: American Gamelan Institute, 1997. Videocassette (VHS), 22 min.

Gogarten, Friedrich. *Christ the Crisis.* Richmond: John Knox, 1972.

Goizueta, Roberto S. "Knowing the God of the Poor: The Preferential Option for the Poor." In *Opting for the Margins: Postmodernity and Liberation in Christian Theology*, edited by Joerg Rieger, 143–56. Oxford: Oxford University Press, 2003.

Gutiérrez, Gustavo. *Gustavo Gutiérrez: Essential Writings.* Edited by James Nicoloff. The Making of Modern Theology. New York: Orbis, 1996.

———. "Liberation Praxis and Christian Faith." In *Frontiers of Theology in Latin America*, edited by Rosino Gibelllini, 1–33. Maryknoll, NY: Orbis, 1979.

———. *A Theology of Liberation: History, Politics, and Salvation.* Maryknoll, NY: Orbis, 2001.

Gramsci, Antonio. *Selections from the Prison Notebooks of Antonio Gramsci.* Edited and Translated by Quiten Hoare and Geoffrey Smith. New York: International, 1973.

Grenz, Stanley J., and Roger E. Olson, *Twentieth-Century Theology: God and the World in a Transitional Age.* Downers Grove, IL: InterVarsity, 1992.

Hall, Stuart. "The West and the Rest: Discourse and Power." In *Formations of Modernity*, edited by Stuart Hall and Bram Gieben, 274–320. Understanding Modern Societies 1. Cambridge: Polity, 1992.

Hardt, Michael, and Antonio Negri. *Empire.* Cambridge: Harvard University Press, 2000.

Harvey, David. *The Condition of Postmodernity.* Cambridge, MA: Blackwell, 1989.

Hauerwas, Stanley. *After Christendom? How the Church Is to Behave if Freedom, Justice, and a Christian Nation Are Bad Ideas.* Nashville: Abingdon, 1991.

Bibliography

Hebblethwaite, Brian. "Incarnation." In *New and Enlarged Handbook of Christian Theology*, edited by Donald W. Musser and Joseph L. Price, 256–60. Nashville: Abingdon, 2003.
Hefner, Robert W. "Of Faith and Commitment: Christian Conversion in Muslim Java." In *Conversion to Christianity: Historical and Anthropological Perspectives on a Great Transformation*, edited by Robert W. Hefner, 99–125. Berkeley: University of California Press, 1993.
Hegel, Georg W. Friedrich. *Lectures on the Philosophy of Religion*. Translated and edited by Peter C. Hodgson et al. 3 vols. Berkeley: University of California Press, 1984.
———. *Phenomenology of Spirit*. Translated by A. V. Miller. Oxford: Clarendon, 1977.
Henry, Patricia B. "The Religion of Balance: Evidence from an Eleventh-Century Javanese Poem." In *Indonesian Religions in Transition*, edited by Rita Smith Kipp and Susan Rodgers Siregar, 72–86. Tucson: University of Arizona Press, 1987.
Hodgson, Peter C. *God in History: Shapes of Freedom*. Nashville: Abingdon, 1989.
———. *New Birth of Freedom: A Theology of Bondage and Liberation*. Philadelphia: Fortress, 1976.
———. *Revisioning the Church: Ecclesial Freedom in the New Paradigm*. Philadelphia: Fortress, 1988.
———. *Winds of the Spirit: A Constructive Christian Theology*. London: SCM, 1994.
hooks, bell. *Talking Back: Thinking Feminist, Thinking Black*. Boston: South End, 1989.
———. *Yearning: Race, Gender, and Cultural Politics*. Women's Studies, Black Studies. Boston: South End, 1990.
Hopkins, Dwight. "More Than Ever: The Preferential Option for the Poor." In *Opting for the Margins: Postmodernity and Liberation in Christian Theology*, edited by Joerg Rieger, 127–42. Oxford: Oxford University Press, 2003.
Isasi-Díaz, Ada María. *Mujerista Theology: A Theology for the Twenty-First Century*. Maryknoll, NY: Orbis, 1996.
Jameson, Frederic. *Postmodernism, or, The Cultural Logic of Late Capitalism*. Durham: Duke University Press, 1991.
JanMohamed, Abdul R. "Some Implications of Paulo Freire's Border Pedagogy." *Cultural Studies* 7 (1993) 107–16.
Käsemann, Ernst. *Perspectives on Paul*. London: SCM, 1971.
Kierkegaard, Søren. "Subjective Truth, Inwardness; Truth Is Subjectivity." In vol. 1 of *Concluding Unscientific Postscripts to*

Bibliography

the Philosophical Fragments, edited and translated by Howard V. Hong and Edna H. Hong, 189–249. Princeton: Princeton University Press, 1992.

Kraemer, Hendrick H. *Religion and the Christian Faith*. Philadelphia: Westminster, 1956.

Lazear, Edward P., editor. *Education in the Twenty-First Century*. Stanford: Hoover Institute, 2002.

Lugones, María. "Playfulness, 'World'-Travelling and Loving Perception." *Hypatia* 2 (1987) 3–19.

Lugones, María, and Elizabeth Spelman. "Have We Got a Theory for You! Feminist Theory, Cultural Imperialism and the Demand for 'the Woman's Voice.'" *Women's Studies International Forum* 6 (1983) 573–81.

Lyotard, Jean-François. *The Postmodern Condition: A Report on Knowledge*. Translated by Geoffrey Bennington. Manchester: Manchester University Press, 1984.

Maldonado-Torres, Nelson. "Liberation Theology and the Search for the Lost Paradigm: From Radical Orthodoxy to Radical Diversality." In *Latin American Liberation Theology: The Next Generation*, edited by Ivan Petrella, 39–61. Maryknoll, NY: Orbis, 2005.

Martin, Biddy, and Chandra Talpade Mohanty. "Feminist Politics: What's Home Got to Do with It?" In *Feminist Studies, Critical Studies*, edited by Theresa De Lauretis, 119–212. Bloomington: Indiana University Press, 1986.

Martínez-Vázquez, Hjamil A. "Breaking the Established Scaffold: Imagination as a Resource in the Development of Biblical Interpretation." In *Her Master's Tools? Feminist and Postcolonial Engagements of Historical-Critical Discourse*. Edited by Caroline Vander Stichele and Todd C. Penner, 71–92. Global Perspectives on Biblical Scholarship 9. Boston: Brill, 2005.

McLaren, Peter L. "Critical Pedagogy: A Look at the Major Concepts." In *The Critical Pedagogy Reader*, edited by Antonia Darder et al., 69–96. New York: Routledge, 2003.

———. *Critical Pedagogy in the New Information Age*. New York: Routledge, 1998.

———. *Life in Schools: An Introduction to Critical Pedagogy in the Foundations of Education*. New York: Longman, 1989.

———. "Postmodernity and the Death of Politics: A Brazilian Reprieve." In *Politics of Liberation: Paths From Freire*, edited by Peter L. McLaren and Colin Lankshear, 193–215. New York: Routledge, 1994.

Bibliography

Metz, Johann Baptist. *Faith in History and Society: Toward a Practical Fundamental Theology*. New York: Crossroad, 2004.
Mignolo, Walter D. *The Darker Side of the Renaissance: Literacy, Territoriality, and Colonization*. Ann Arbor: University of Michigan Press, 1995.
———. *Local Histories/Global Designs: Coloniality, Subaltern Knowledges, and Border Thinking*. Princeton: Princeton University Press, 2000.
Minh-Ha, Trinh. *Woman, Native, Other: Writing Postcoloniality and Feminism*. Bloomington: Indiana University Press, 1989.
Moltmann, Jürgen. *The Church in the Power of the Spirit: A Contribution to Messianic Ecclesiology*. Translated by Margaret Kohl. New York: Harper & Row, 1977.
———. *The Coming of God: Christian Eschatology*. Translated by Margaret Kohl. Minneapolis: Fortress, 1996.
———. *The Crucified God: The Cross of Christ as the Foundation and Criticism of Christian Theology*. Translated by R. A. Wilson and John Bowden. Minneapolis: Fortress, 1993.
———. *The Source of Life: The Holy Spirit and the Theology of Life*. Translated by Margaret Kohl. Minneapolis: Fortress, 1997.
———. *Theology of Hope: On the Ground and the Implications of a Christian Eschatology*. Translated by J. W. Leitch. London: SCM, 1967.
———. *Theology Today: Two Contributions Towards Making Theology Present*. Translated by John Bowden. London: SCM, 1988.
Moore, Robert L. "Space and Transformation in Human Experience." In *Anthropology and the Study of Religion*, edited by Robert L. Moore and Frank Reynolds, 96–114. Studies in Religion and Society. Chicago: Center for the Scientific Study of Religion, 1984.
Mouffe, Chantal. "Hegemony and Ideology in Gramsci." In *Gramsci and Marxist Theory*, edited by Chantal Mouffe, 168–204. London: Routledge & Kegan Paul, 1979.
Mudge, Lewis S. *Rethinking the Beloved Community: Ecclesiology, Hermeneutics, Social Theory*. Lanham, MD: University Press of America, 1992.
———. *Sense of a People: Toward a Church for the Human Future*. Philadelphia: Trinity International, 1992.
Munslow, Alun. *The Routledge Companion to Historical Studies*. London: Routledge, 2000.
Naas, Michael. *Derrida from Now On*. Perspectives in Continental Philosophy. Bronx, NY: Fordham University Press, 2008.

Bibliography

Niebuhr, Reinhold. *Moral Man and Immoral Society: A Study in Ethics and Politics*. Library of Theological Ethics. Louisville: Westminster John Knox, 2011.

Pemberton, John. "Disorienting Culturalist Assumptions: A View from 'Java.'" In *In Near Ruins: Cultural Theory at the End of the Century*, edited by Nicholas B. Dirks, 119–46. Minneapolis: University of Minnesota Press, 1998.

———. *On the Subject of "Java."* Ithaca: Cornell University Press, 1994.

Perez, Emma. *The Decolonial Imaginary: Writing Chicanas into History.* Bloomington: Indiana University Press, 1999.

Petrella, Ivan. *The Future of Liberation Theology: An Argument and Manifesto*. Burlington, VT: Ashgate, 2004.

Pui-lan, Kwok. *Introducing Asian Feminist Theology*. Introductions in Feminist Theology 4. Cleveland: Pilgrim, 2000.

———. "Jesus/The Native: Biblical Studies from a Postcolonial Perspective." In *Teaching the Bible: The Discourses and Politics of Biblical Pedagogy*, edited by Fernando F. Segovia and Mary Ann Tolbert, 69–85. Maryknoll, NY: Orbis, 1998.

———. "The Mission of God in Asia and Theological Education." *Ministerial Formation* 48 (1990) 23–35.

———. "Postcolonial Imagination: Historical, Dialogical, and Diasporic." In *Postcolonial Imagination and Feminist Theology*, 29–51. Louisville: Westminster John Knox, 2005.

———. "The Sources and Resources of Feminist Theologies: A Post-Colonial Perspective." In *Sources and Resources of Feminist Theologies*, edited by Elizabeth Hartlieb and Charlotte Methuen, 5–23. Yearbook of the European Society of Women in Theological Research 5. Kampen, Netherlands: Kok Pharos, 1997.

———, editor. *Discovering the Bible in the Non-Biblical World.* The Bible and Liberation Series. Maryknoll, NY: Orbis, 1995.

Richard, Pablo. *Death of Christendoms, Birth of the Church: Historical Analysis and Theological Interpretation of the Church in Latin America*. Maryknoll, NY: Orbis, 1987.

———. "Liberation Theology Today: Crisis or Challenge?" *Envio* 133 (1992) 24–31.

Ritschl, Albrecht. *The Christian Doctrine of Justification and Reconciliation: The Positive Development of the Doctrine*. 2nd edition. Edited by H.R. Mackintosh and A.B. Macaulay. Edinburgh: T. & T. Clark, 1902.

Bibliography

Ruether, Rosemary R., and Rosemary Skinner, editors. *Women and Religion in America: A Documentary History*. 3 vols. New York: Harper & Row, 1981–1985.

Russell, Letty. *Church in the Round: Feminist Interpretation of the Church*. Louisville: Westminster John Knox, 1993.

Said, Edward. *Culture and Imperialism*. New York: Vintage, 1993.

———. *Orientalism*. London: Vintage, 1978.

Saldíva-Hull, Sonia. *Feminism on the Border: Chicana Gender Politics and Literature*. Berkeley: University of California Press, 2000.

Schmitt, Carl. *Political Theology: Four Chapters on the Concept of Sovereignty*. Translated by George Schwab. Chicago: Chicago University Press, 2005.

Schweitzer, Albert. *The Quest of the Historical Jesus*. Edited by John Bowden. Minneapolis: Fortress, 2001.

Sears, Laurie J. *Shadows of Empire: Colonial Discourse and Javanese Tales*. Durham: Duke University Press, 1996.

Segovia, Fernando F., editor. *Interpreting Beyond Borders*. Bible and Postcolonialism 3. Sheffield, UK: Sheffield Academic, 2000.

Shor, Ira, and Paulo Freire. "What Is the 'Dialogical Method' of Teaching?" *Journal of Education* 169 (1987) 11–31.

Simon, Roger. "Empowerment as a Pedagogy of Possibility." *Language Arts* 64 (1987) 370–82.

———. *Teaching Against the Grain: Texts for a Pedagogy of Possibility*. Critical Studies in Education and Culture. New York: Bergin & Garvey, 1992.

Söelle, Dorothee. *Political Theology*. Philadelphia: Fortress, 1974.

Spinoza, Benedictus de. *Theological-Political Treatise*. 2nd ed. Translated by Samuel Shirley. Indianapolis: Hackett, 2001.

Spivak, Gayatri Chakravorty. *A Critique of Postcolonial Reason: Toward a History of the Vanishing Present*. Cambridge: Harvard University Press, 1999.

———. *In Other Worlds: Essays in Cultural Politics*. New York: Routledge, 2006.

Spivak, Gayatri Chakravorty, and Sarah Harasym. *The Post-Colonial Critic: Interviews, Strategies, Dialogues*. New York, Routledge, 1990.

Taylor, Mark Lewis. "Subalternity and Advocacy as Kairos for Theology." In *Opting for the Margins: Postmodernity and Liberation in Christian Theology*, edited by Joerg Rieger, 24–44. Oxford: Oxford University Press, 2003.

Bibliography

Taubes, Jacob. *The Political Theology of Paul.* Edited by Aleida Assmann et al. and translated by Dana Hollander. Stanford: Stanford University Press, 2004.

Tillich, Paul. *Dynamics of Faith.* Vol. 10 of World Perspectives. New York: Harper, 1957.

———. *Systematic Theology.* Vol. 2, *Existence and the Christ.* Chicago: University of Chicago Press, 1957.

Troeltsch, Ernst. *The Christian Faith.* Translated by Garrett E. Paul. Minneapolis: Fortress, 1991.

———. *Writings on Theology and Religion.* Translated and edited by Robert Morgan and Michael Pye. Louisville: Westminster John Knox, 1990.

Turner, Victor W. "Betwixt and Between: The Liminal Period in Rites of Passage." In *Symposium on New Approaches to the Study of Religion*, proceedings of the 1964 Annual Spring Meeting of the American Ethnological Society, edited by June Helms, 4–20. Seattle: University of Washington Press, 1964.

———. *Dramas, Fields, and Metaphors: Symbolic Action in Human Society.* Symbol, Myth, and Ritual Series. Ithaca: Cornell University Press, 1974.

———. *The Drums of Affliction: A Study of Religious Processes among the Ndembu of Zambia.* International African Institute. Oxford: Clarendon, 1968.

———. *From Ritual to Theatre: The Human Seriousness of Play.* Vol. 1 of Performance Studies Series. New York: Performing Arts Journal Publications, 1982.

———. *The Ritual Process: Structure and Anti-Structure.* Lewis Henry Morgan Lecture, 1966. Chicago: Aldine, 1969.

Watson, Keith. *Education in the Third World.* London: Croom Helm, 1982.

Weber, Max. *The Protestant Ethic and the Spirit of Capitalism.* Translated by Talcott Parsons. London: Routledge, 1930.

Weiler, Kathleen. *Women Teaching for Change: Gender, Class, and Power.* Critical Studies in Education. South Hadley, MA: Bergin & Garvey, 1988.

Weiss, Johannes. *Jesus' Proclamation of the Kingdom of God.* Lives of Jesus. Philadelphia: Fortress, 1971.

Welch, Sharon D. *Communities of Resistance and Solidarity: A Feminist Theology of Liberation.* Maryknoll, NY: Orbis, 1985.

White, Hayden V. *The Content of the Form: Narrative Discourse and Historical Representation.* Baltimore: John Hopkins University Press, 1987.

Bibliography

Yewangoe, Andreas A. *Theologia Crucis in Asia: Asian Christian Views on Suffering in the Face of Overwhelming Poverty and Multifaceted Religiosity in Asia.* Amsterdam: Rodopi, 1987.

www.ingramcontent.com/pod-product-compliance
Lightning Source LLC
Chambersburg PA
CBHW071440160426
43195CB00013B/1979